Making Gingerbread Houses

For my Nan, Betty Emmerton.
Thank you.

Making Gingerbread Houses

Candice Clayton

NEW HOLLAND

William Shakespere wrote: 'And I had but one penny in the world, thou should'st have it to buy gingerbread.'

CONTENTS

INTRODUCTION

Who doesn't love a gingerbread house at Christmas?!

Welcome to Making Gingerbread Houses, a complete guide to gingerbread house construction and design. With flavorful recipes, hints, tips and projects for every skill level, I hope you find the magical gingerbread houses of your dreams within these pages.

Gingerbread is traditionally associated with Christmas because of its origins, but this beloved classic shouldn't be confined to the festive season. Bring the flavor and delight of gingerbread houses out of Christmas to be enjoyed all year round by incorporating it into other celebrations. The Bird House (on page 45) is perfect for baby showers and kitchen teas, the Easter Bunny House (on page 79) is spot on for time and even design your own haunted house for Halloween!

You will notice through the book a lot of my houses have minimal lolly decorations and fondant coverings on them – this is because I want you to see the gingerbread and give you an idea of how to decorate it. Adapt and change these designs to suit your taste and style, and make them your own. After all, eating and enjoying your gingerbread masterpiece is the best part!

These days houses look very different, with a lot more high density and minimalistic living spaces I love the idea of creating a Christmas gingerbread house that reflects the architecture of your neighborhood, home town or even a replica of your own home or school.

Remember, your gingerbread house doesn't need to pass a real housing inspection or be an award winner to be awesome, the spirit of the season should be the focus of your creation.

So, gather your friends, family and supplies and enjoy the creative process of making something artistic and delicious.

Happy baking!

Candice X

GINGERBREAD BASES

A note on gluten-free: All of the recipes in this book can be made gluten-free by simply substituting plain flour for gluten-free flour.

RECIPE #1: LIGHT, CRISP AND SUBTLE

This is very light tasting gingerbread with not a lot of oomph to the flavor. It's suitable for those who are not huge fans of a strong gingerbread taste. While initially this gingerbread can seem quite bland, the taste sneaks up on you after a few pieces.

Use for: Gingerbread house construction, individual biscuits that will be iced or heavily decorated. This recipe isn't too soft or doughy so has less risk of breaking.

> TIP: Ensure your butter is soft, at room temperature or slightly softer so that it holds its shape but would be difficult to pick up with your fingers, this allows it to easily emulsify with your sugar and ensures no lumpy bits.

You will need
125g (4oz) unsalted butter, softened at room temperature
100g (3.5oz) light Muscovado natural unrefined cane sugar
1 egg yolk
480g (17oz) plain flour
3 heaped tsp ginger spice powder
1 pinch baking powder
125ml (4fl oz) maple syrup

Method
- Sift together your dry ingredients in a medium mixing bowl.
- Using electric beaters, cream the butter and sugar together. Once mixed, add in the egg yolk and mix until well combined.
- Add the rest of the ingredients, mixing on low while adding ¼ of the Maple syrup and ⅓ of the dry ingredients. Alternate between the two until finished.

- Once the mixture forms a crumbly dough, bring your dough onto your bench and knead it together to form a ball. Allow the dough to sit for 10 minutes, while you line a baking tray with baking paper.
- Roll the dough onto the baking paper lined tray to bake as a solid sheet or roll out and cut shapes before baking. (For more on this, see page 23.)

Baking: Bake in the middle of the oven for 10 minutes* at 150°C/ 300°F.

> TIP: Using light, unrefined cane sugar in this recipe is great because it has a very unobtrusive flavor and it is not sickly sweet – this helps to create the overall subtle flavor of this gingerbread. It also has a smooth texture, which gives a nice strong structure to the bread.

RECIPE #2: SOFT AND FLUFFY, RICH AND DARK

This is a very rich tasting gingerbread with a rich mahogany color and smokey aroma. The dark muscovado sugar and golden syrup combine to create gingerbread with a kick. The rich flavors of this recipe lend itself to the potential for the addition of strong spices, if you were considering experimenting with spice this is the recipe to do it, as the strong spice will compliment, not overpower the overall taste of the gingerbread.

Use for: Individual biscuits. This recipe is too soft and doughy for gingerbread house construction. It has a high risk of breaking due to the softness of the honey and golden syrup.

> **TIP:** If you like dark muscovado and want to make a house out of it, simply use 1 cup of maple syrup instead of golden syrup or maple and honey together – but remember this will change the overall taste and color of your gingerbread.

> **TIP:** *Oven temperatures vary and an increase or decrease in recipe size will affect your cooking time. Get to know your oven and always keep an eye on it while baking.

You will need

250g (8oz) unsalted butter, softened
200g (7oz) dark Muscovado natural unrefined cane sugar
2 egg yolks
480g (17oz) plain flour
5 heaped tsp ginger spice powder
1 pinch baking powder
250ml (8fl oz) golden syrup
OR
140g (5oz) maple syrup and
140g (5oz) of honey

Method

- Pre-sift your dry ingredients together in a medium sized mixing bowl.
- Using electric beaters, cream the butter and sugar together until well mixed. Once creamed, add in the egg yolks and beat until the mixture is completely blended.
- Add the rest of the ingredients, mixing on low while adding ¼ of the golden syrup and ⅓ of the dry ingredients. Alternate between the two until finished.
- Bring your dough onto your bench and knead it together to form a ball. Leave it to sit for 10 minutes, while you line a baking tray with baking paper.
- Roll the dough onto the baking paper lined tray to bake as a solid sheet or roll out and cut shapes before baking. (For more on this see page 23.)

Baking: Bake in the middle of the oven for 15-17 minutes* at 150°C/ 300°F. This is a sugar heavy recipe of dense ingredients and so it will take a little longer to cook.

> **TIP:** Using a dark unrefined cane sugar is a great addition as it contains a bit more molasses, which results in a darker color, softer texture and rich complex taste.

RECIPE #3: TROPICANA

Who doesn't like ginger and glazed fruit pieces at Christmas? I certainly do, so the idea of turning this flavor sensation into a gingerbread recipe was too good to pass up. Ginger-pineapple is my favorite, but you can substitute the fruit juice of any fruit you like to suit your tastes! This recipe gives an immediate flavor burst upon eating with a sweet fruity taste that lingers on the palate. It is fantastic served with soft cheeses.

Use for: Gingerbread house construction or individual biscuits. This recipe isn't too soft or doughy so has less risk of crumbling. It will go slightly crisper than traditional soft gingerbreads.

You will need
125g (4oz) unsalted butter (softened)
110g (4oz) dark brown sugar
1 egg yolk
480g (17oz) plain flour
3 heaped teaspoon ginger spice powder
1 pinch baking powder
125ml (4fl oz) pineapple juice

Method
- Pre-sift your dry ingredients together in a medium sized mixing bowl.
- Using electric beaters, cream the butter and sugar together until well mixed. Once creamed, add in the egg yolks and beat until the mixture is completely blended.
- Add in half of your pineapple juice and mix until clear, then add half of your dry ingredients, slowly, and mix until all clear. Add your remaining juice, once combined slowly add the remaining dry ingredients.

- Bring your dough onto your bench and knead it together to form a ball. Leave it to sit for 10 minutes, while you line a baking tray with baking paper.
- Roll the dough onto the baking paper lined tray to bake as a solid sheet or roll out and cut shapes before baking. (For more on this see page 23.)

Baking: Bake in the middle of the oven for 15 minutes* at 150°C/ 300°F.

TIP: If you get a bit carried away with adding juice and your mix is very wet and not a dough-like consistency – add 1 tablespoon of cornflour at a time, mixing it in thoroughly before each addition until it thickens up. If you add too much you may need to consider adding an additional egg yolk to ensure structure.

RECIPE #4: GINGER APPLE-CINNAMON.

Ginger and cinnamon are two spice flavors that work together nicely. Apple and cinnamon is a much-loved combination in many dishes, and the addition of ginger really makes this a subtle, warming gingerbread.

Use for: Gingerbread house construction or individual biscuits. This recipe is soft and doughy due to the apple sauce, while it doesn't have a tendency to crumble, be sure to coat the back of any bread piece that is used as larger construction pieces to avoid the risk of crumbling and collapsing the structure.

You will need

125g (4oz) unsalted butter, softened
110g (4oz) dark brown sugar
1 egg yolk
430g (15oz) plain flour
3 heaped teaspoons ginger spice powder or 1 tablespoon ginger syrup
2–3 heaped teaspoon cinnamon spice powder/ cinnamon sugar
90ml (3fl oz) apple sauce

Method

- Pre-sift your dry ingredients together in a medium sized mixing bowl.
- Using electric beaters, cream the butter and sugar together until well mixed. Once creamed, add in the egg yolks and beat until the mixture is completely blended.
- Add in the dry ingredients and apple sauce slowly, starting with the apple sauce, then the dry ingredients. Repeat until all dry ingredients and apple sauce are mixed in. The mixture should look like a wet, well-combined doughy substance.
- Bring your dough onto your bench and knead it together to form a ball. Leave it to sit for 10 minutes, while you line a baking tray with baking paper.
- Roll the dough onto the baking paper lined tray to bake as a solid sheet or roll out and cut shapes before baking. (For more on this see page 23.)

Baking: Bake in the middle of the oven for 15 minutes* at 150°C/ 300°F.

RECIPE #5: GINGER-CHILI-CHOCOLATE

The ginger spice is less obvious in this recipe. It is more of a lingering background spice adding warmth and depth to a dominant chocolate taste with a chili kick. This recipe yields very dark, almost black looking bread which contrasts nicely with white chocolate or royal icing. (See the Russian Dollhouse on page 71.)

Use for: Gingerbread house construction or individual biscuits. This recipe is firm and eats more like a brownie. It doesn't have a tendency to crumble so is great for gingerbread house construction.

You will need

250g (8oz) unsalted butter, softened
220g (8oz) dark brown sugar
2 egg yolks
670g (23.5oz) plain flour
6 teaspoons ginger spice
1½ – 2 teaspoons of chili jam or 3 teaspoons of dry chili flakes
150g (5oz) dark or milk chocolate – melt it down after weighing
70ml (2.5fl oz) of maple syrup

A note on chocolate: I use a basic compound chocolate from the baking section of the supermarket or cake decorating supply store. You don't want anything too high in milk fat, as it doesn't cook as well, so keep your yummy bars and expensive balls of chocolate in the cupboard for eating while you are baking!

Method

- Pre-sift your dry ingredients together in a medium sized mixing bowl.
- Using electric beaters, cream the butter and sugar together until well mixed. Once creamed, add in the egg yolks and the chili jam and beat until the mixture is completely blended.
- Add in the dry ingredients and maple slowly, starting with the maple syrup, then the dry ingredients. Repeat until all dry ingredients and maple syrup are mixed in. The mixture should look like a wet, well-combined doughy substance.
- Add in the 125g (4oz) of melted chocolate and mix until clear.
- Bring your dough onto your bench and roll it out immediately as you don't want the chocolate to reach room temperature.

Baking: Bake in the middle of the oven for 15 minutes* at 150°C/ 300°F.

> **TIP:** Be careful of this recipe – it will not be forgiving of a slight over bake – over baked versions of this are dry and very hard. The chocolate sets fast, so either work faster or halve the recipe to make two batches at seperate times.

RECIPE #6: CHEATS CARAMELIZED GINGER

Soft, smooth and subtle. A gentle hint of caramel in a smooth medium brown gingerbread, with ginger the predominant but not overpowering flavor in this medium strength recipe is bound to be a hit with the whole family.

Use for: Gingerbread house construction or individual biscuits. This recipe is soft but sturdy in texture. Reinforce the back of structural pieces with a salted caramel chocolate to ensure no breakages.

You will need

250g (8oz) unsalted butter, softened
220g (8oz) dark brown sugar
2 egg yolks
670g (23.5oz) plain flour
6 teaspoons ginger spice
140g (5oz) of super thick caramel sauce
70g (2.5oz) of maple syrup

Method

- Pre-sift your dry ingredients together in a medium sized mixing bowl.
- Using electric beaters, cream the butter and sugar together until well mixed. Once creamed, add in the egg yolks and beat until the mixture is completely blended.
- Add in the dry ingredients and maple syrup, starting with the maple syrup, then the dry ingredients. Mix until well combined. The mixture should look like a wet, well-combined doughy substance. Add in 125g (4oz) of caramel sauce and mix until clear.

- Bring your dough onto your bench and knead it together to form a ball. Leave it to sit for 10 minutes, while you line a baking tray with baking paper.
- Roll the dough onto the baking paper lined tray to bake as a solid sheet or roll out and cut shapes before baking. (For more on this see page 23.)

Baking: Bake in the middle of the oven for 20 minutes* at 150°C/ 300°F.

TIP: If you want to make this a little more savory and like a hint of salted caramel, add a sprinkle of fresh ground sea salt to the batter.

RECIPE #7: NUTMEG GINGERBREAD

The taste and smell of Christmas! This recipe yields soft bread full of traditional flavor. The golden syrup provides depth while the caster sugar subtly steps aside and lets the warming ginger and the festive taste and aroma of nutmeg shine through.

Use for: Gingerbread house construction only if it has been reinforced with chocolate or toffee backing and individual biscuits cut post baking as the golden syrup allows this batter to spread.

You will need

125g (4oz) unsalted butter, softened
115g (4oz) caster sugar
1 egg yolk
290-390g (10-13oz) plain flour*
3 teaspoons ginger spice
3 teaspoons nutmeg spice
120g (4oz) of golden syrup

Method

- Pre-sift your dry ingredients together in a medium sized mixing bowl.
- Using electric beaters, cream the butter and sugar together until well mixed. Once creamed, add in the egg yolks and beat until the mixture is completely blended.
- Alternate the addition of the dry ingredient and the golden syrup starting with the golden syrup, then the dry ingredients. Repeat until all dry ingredients and golden syrup are mixed in. The mixture should look like a wet, well-combined doughy substance.

- Bring your dough onto your bench and knead it together to form a ball. Leave it to sit for 10 minutes, while you line a baking tray with baking paper.
- Roll the dough onto the baking paper lined tray to bake as a solid sheet or roll out and cut shapes before baking. (For more on this see page 23.)

Baking: Bake in the middle of the oven for 15-20 minutes* at 150°C/ 300°F.

TIP: Asses the wetness of the batter – if it looks more like cake batter, wetter than dough – add an additional 100-125g (3.5-4oz) of plain flour, adding small portions at a time to bring it back to a dough like consistency. Golden syrup is a wonderfully great taste but needs to be handled with care in getting the batter consistency right.

RECIPE #8: SIMPLY SWEET; TRIED AND TRUE

This is a light, subtle tasting gingerbread made for its easy-to-eat delicate flavor and its general all purpose sturdiness.

Use for: Gingerbread house construction or individual biscuits. This recipe is my go-to recipe for all things gingerbread, especially construction and pre-cut cookies.

You will need

250g (8oz) unsalted butter, softened
110g (3.8oz) dark brown sugar
2 egg yolks
765g (27oz) plain flour
5 heaped teaspoons ginger spice powder
275g (10oz) maple syrup

Method

- Pre-sift your dry ingredients together in a medium sized mixing bowl.
- Using electric beaters, cream the butter and sugar together until well mixed. Once creamed, add in the egg yolks and beat until the mixture is completely blended.
- Alternate the addition of the dry ingredient and the maple syrup starting with the maple syrup, then the dry ingredients. Repeat until all dry ingredients and maple syrup are mixed in. The mixture should look like a wet, well-combined doughy substance.

- Bring your dough onto your bench and knead it together to form a ball. Leave it to sit for 10 minutes, while you line a baking tray with baking paper.
- Roll the dough onto the baking paper lined tray to bake as a solid sheet or roll out and cut shapes before baking. (For more on this see page 23.)

Baking: Bake in the middle of the oven for 10-15 minutes* at 150°C/ 300°F.

TIP: Maple syrup is great for this recipe as it isn't as runny as golden syrup and the sugar content is (marginally) lower, which means it isn't as soft and sticky and it isn't as likely to spread when I bake it. Also, because it is thicker with less sugar – the end product is not as soft so it can be used to make walls and roofs that take weight for example.

RECIPE #9: COCONUT AND GINGERBREAD

Coconut is the dominant flavor here with ginger playing a supporting role, providing variety and depth to the overall flavor of the bread. Up your ginger content or add additional spices for variety if you want to balance out the coconut flavor. The bread itself is drier and rougher to the taste than the other recipes owing to the coarse nature of the coconut.

Use for: Gingerbread house construction or individual biscuits both plain and iced or heavily decorated. This recipe yields a textured bread surface not super smooth for fine icing work.

You will need
145ml (5fl oz) coconut oil
60g (2oz) coconut sugar
180g (6oz) coconut flour
1 egg yolk
1 whole egg
3 heaped teaspoons ginger spice powder

Add additional spices to taste – consider something tart like dry cranberries.

Method
- Combine the oil and sugar in your mixing bowl until well combined.
- Add half of the flour and mix until combined.
- Add the whole egg and egg yolk and mix until combined
- Add in the remaining flour and mix well on high for 1–2 minutes until it starts to look a little creamy. The dough in the bowl will not look like it has come together in one piece – you need to knead it on your bench to bring it together.

- Bring your dough onto your bench and knead it together to form a ball. Leave it to sit for 10 minutes, while you line a baking tray with baking paper.
- Roll the dough onto the baking paper lined tray to bake as a solid sheet or roll out and cut shapes before baking. (For more on this see page 23.)

Baking: Bake in the middle of the oven for 15 minutes* at 150°C/ 300°F.

RECIPE #10: VERY VANILLA GINGERBREAD (WITH OPTIONAL BRANDY!)

A surprisingly subtle flavor, perfect for those who don't like a lot of ginger, the addition of brandy is both a warming and delightful treat, with the vanilla really bringing out the brandy flavor and the ginger adding complexity and warmth to the overall taste. Especially nice served with custard or rice pudding.

Use for: A great sturdy structure to use for construction pieces as well as plain or iced cookies.

You will need

125g (4oz) unsalted butter, softened
30g (1oz) vanilla bean sugar (or flavored caster sugar)
1 egg yolk
1 teaspoon vanilla extract
430g (15oz) plain flour
3 heaped teaspoons ginger spice powder or 30ml (1fl oz) ginger syrup
125g (4oz) golden syrup
2 tablespoons brandy, to taste*

Method

- Pre-sift your dry ingredients together in a medium sized mixing bowl.
- Using electric beaters, cream the butter and sugar together until well mixed. Once creamed, add in the egg yolks and vanilla extract and beat until the mixture is completely blended.
- Add in half of the dry ingredients first and mix until well combined. Add all of the golden syrup, mixing well, when clear add the remaining dry ingredients and mix well.

- The dough in the bowl will not look like it has come to together in one piece – bring your dough onto your bench and knead it to bring it together and form a ball. Leave it to sit for 10 minutes, while you line a baking tray with baking paper.
- Roll the dough onto the baking paper lined tray to bake as a solid sheet or roll out and cut shapes before baking. (For more on this see page 23.)

Baking: Bake in the middle of the oven for 15 minutes* at 150°C/ 300°F.

TIP: *If you add more than this you need to add a bit of extra flour to compensate for the additional liquid. If you start to be so generous as to measure this in ¼ cups then add an extra egg to keep it all bound together!

CHOCOLATE BARK

Chocolate bark is a simple and delicious treat that is easy to make – it consists of melted chocolate loaded up with small or crushed ingredients like sweet pizza toppings that give it a pop of texture and color. The additions are limited to your imagination.

You will need
Chocolate of your choice (if using to reinforce structural house pieces use standard compound chocolate).

Additional pieces of flavor/texture as required (crushed peppermint candy canes, crushed hazelnut pieces, sprinkles, small chocolates, crushed cookie or dried fruit pieces).

Optional
Oil based (chocolate) food color
Oil based (chocolate) food flavor

Method
- Pre-prepare a cookie sheet by lining it with baking paper.
- Place your chocolate in a heat proof bowl over a pot of simmering water and stir the chocolate continuously until it is melted. If you are going to add one color or flavor – add it now as the chocolate is melting and make sure it is mixed in thoroughly.
- Pour the melted chocolate into the cookie tray as evenly as possible and smooth it out gently with a silicon spatula.

- Once the chocolate is in the tray quickly and evenly add in any textured pieces to the top of the chocolate.
- Once the base of the tray is cool enough to be touched with a flat hand, place the tray in the refrigerator for up to an hour to allow the chocolate to set.
- Once the chocolate sets you roughly break the chocolate apart with your hands, giving hap hazard shards of rough surfaced chocolate that looks just like sugar 'bark'.

TIPS: Pair up complementary flavors like dark chocolate and chilli or white chocolate and raspberries. For a Christmas theme – crush up some candy canes! For try out mixing orange and purple color chocolate and add in small candy eye balls.

If you are melting white chocolate and mixing two different colors and flavors, do so as soon as the chocolate is melted. Take a fork or bread knife and swirl it around on the tray to mix in the color in a marbled pattern.

If you are applying the chocolate bark to the back of a gingerbread cookie or construction, apply the melted chocolate directly onto the back of the gingerbread and sprinkle a thin layer of texture pieces over the top before leaving for at least an hour at room temperature to set.

If you want to cut shapes out of your bark, follow the steps above but instead of putting the bark in refrigerator, allow the chocolate to start setting at room temperature – when it is set enough to hold its shape (not runny) but is not yet hard, use a lightly spray-oiled cookie cutter to cut out your shapes. Cut out the shapes but leave them in place.

If you want to curl the edges – gently do so with your fingers now. Once you have cut all of your shapes out place the tray in the fridge for 30-45 minutes or until set hard. Once the chocolate is set, remove all of your scrap pieces from the tray first and then peel the baking paper off of the back of your chocolate shapes. This is a great option for green trees with sprinkles for ornaments and chocolate-brown fences.

ROYAL ICING

You will need
500g (1lb) pure icing sugar
75g (3oz) egg white
Lemon juice

Method
- Double sift the icing sugar into a mixing bowl, add in the egg whites and mix on a low-medium setting until the mix forms peaks.

Note: This recipe is courtesy of The Northern Sydney Institute, part of TAFE NSW.

SUGAR/SYRUP	COLOR	TASTE
Caster Sugar	White	Sweet and light, unobtrusive
Raw Sugar	Beige/light brown	Not as sweet as white sugar
Brown Sugar	Golden brown	Less sweet than white, deep, rich flavor shows through but is not dominating
Dark Brown Sugar	Rich deep brown	Deep rich flavor that holds its own when mixed with spices without taking over
Light Muscovado	Beige/light brown	Light and sweet
Dark Muscovado	Deep mahogany brown	Deep rich flavor that holds its own when mixed with spices
Vanilla Bean sugar	Beige/off white in color	Light and sweet with heavy overtones of vanilla
Coconut sugar	Beige/off white in color	Light and sweet with heavy overtones of coconut
Icing Sugar	White	Super sweet
Maple Syrup	Deep rich golden brown in color	Tasted on its own it is very sweet and strong in maple flavor – baked it is subtly sweet and provides a smoky taste in the background of other spices present
Golden Syrup	Light rich gold color	Rich, strong sweet flavor that makes its presence known, regardless of other ingredient. Combined with spices this provides a full body of flavors
Honey	Light rich gold color	Tasted on its own it is a strong, complex dominating flavor, baked it provides sweetness but the honey flavor is usually an aftertaste

TEXTURE	HOW IT BAKES	GOOD FOR HOUSE CONSTRUCTION	GOOD FOR PRE-CUT INDIVIDUAL BISCUITS
Fine granules	Light-golden and quickly	Yes	Yes – if refrigerated first
Medium refined granules – requires more emulsification time with the butter in step 1	Golden in color and fairly quickly	Yes	Yes – if refrigerated first
Course, slightly sticky fine granules	Golden brown in color and fairly quickly	Yes	Yes – if refrigerated first
Course, rough feeling, wet-ish fine granules	Deep rich brown in color	Yes	Yes – if refrigerated first
Course, slightly sticky fine granules	Golden, light beige in color	Yes	Yes – if refrigerated first
Course, slightly sticky fine granules	Mahogany brown in color	Yes	Yes – if refrigerated first
Course, less refined granules – requires more emulsification time with the butter	Golden, light beige in color	Yes	Yes – if refrigerated first
Coarse, less refined granules – requires more emulsification time with the butter	Golden, light toasted brown in color	Yes	Yes – if refrigerated first
Fine powder	Takes on the color of the mixture	Less so if it is the only sugar present as it has no bulk to it	Yes – if refrigerated first
Pours easy, thick consistency	Provides an undertone of rich brown	Yes	Yes – if refrigerated first
Pours easy – thin consistency	Gives a deep, rich golden toasted color	No	Not pre-cut shapes. Cut post baking is a better option
Difficulty to pour, very thick	Provides a golden undertone	No	Yes – if refrigerated first not as secure as other sugars

HINTS AND TIPS: INGREDIENTS, RECIPES AND BAKING

- Is the recipe you have chosen for structure or taste not as golden as you wanted? Don't worry – there is always a solution. To achieve a nice golden color, add one drop of egg-yellow and one drop of orange gel-food color for every two drops of chocolate brown color. You won't need much to get to that perfect shade.

- Save time and money when you separate your eggs to use the yolks for your gingerbread – keep your egg whites together in a small bowl in the fridge – you will need these to make your royal icing when you construct your gingerbread house! Be sure to use your egg whites within 24 hours though otherwise you may want to consider freezing them in ice cube trays and defrosting them when you are ready to make your royal icing.

- Cornflour is a cure-all. If you ever have a slip of the hand with your wet ingredients, don't throw your mix out, mix in what you have and assess how wet the dough is – at the end of adding ingredients and mixing well if it is still too wet – add a small amount of cornflour, small bits at a time.

- If you ever find yourself out of ginger spice powder, you can use ginger syrup instead! But remember it is a liquid, so you will need to adjust your recipe to make sure that your dry:wet ingredient ratio is balanced. Gingerbread with syrup in it it is more likely to spread when baked, so if you are going to use ginger syrup for individual cookies, do a quick test of one or two pre-cut shapes in the oven and if they spread too much use the cut-after-bake, method described on page 23.

- Deal with fussy eaters by creating soft and fluffy gingerbread cakes sure to please the fussiest eater! Use self-raising flour and golden syrup and cut the shapes after baking (see page 23) to create a lovely soft, fluffy cake like gingerbread. This type of cake is completely useless for construction but perfect for those with a preference for the softer textures for eating.

- What makes a chewy gingerbread? Molasses. Molasses comes in a variety of different forms – choose one that suits you, but Molasses more than honey gives chewy soft bread. Be careful however you can't have your chewy bread and avoid spread too! Molasses will cause your dough to spread even if you refrigerate it first, so reconsider using it for fine, fiddly shapes or cut shapes from a sheet post baking.

TECHNIQUES

ROLLING OUT AND CUTTING YOUR SHAPES: THREE OPTIONS

Everyone has a different method that they swear works perfectly. I have found that there are three options and all of them work well when paired with the recipe type that requires it.

The make-rest, roll-rest, cut-rest, bake Method: (The 4-step work and rest method)
This is the most common method used when making a large number of novelty shaped cookies for decoration. It works really well if you are using a recipe that is not high in butter or fat and uses a sugar and syrup that doesn't melt quickly and therefore won't spread out of shape. To execute this Method:
* Make your dough and leave it to rest in the fridge for at least 20 minutes.
* Roll out the dough and leave it to rest in the fridge for at least 20 minutes.
* Cut out the dough into the desired shapes and leave the uncooked cookies in the fridge to rest for at least 20 minutes/until they reach the fridge tempertaure, although overnight is ideal.
* Once rested, remove the cookies from the fridge and place them directly into a preheated oven and bake.

> **TIP:** Don't worry if your tray pops out of place when you take it out of the fridge, this is a common occurrence. Don't use this method for precisely measured pieces.

The dough-in-the-fridge-over-night Method: (The overnight method)
A slightly different take on the 4 step work and rest method, this method involves making the dough and leaving it to rest in the fridge overnight before rolling it out, cutting out shapes and baking the next day. Be sure to rest the dough shapes in the fridge for at least 20 minutes/until they reach fridge temperate again before baking to minimize spread.

The bake-a-sheet and cut shapes after baking method
The quickest of all three methods and therefore the preferred method of the impatient baker like myself. To execute this method you rollout your freshly made dough onto cookie sheets – place them in the fridge to get cool and a bit hard and bring them out, place the cookie cutter/template over the cold dough and roughly mark out around the area in which you will cut out your shape cut away any excess from the sides and center of gingerbread that isn't going to be used in your shapes and return these pieces to the left over dough to be reused again.

You are leaving a small edge of gingerbread that is going to be cut away when you cut your shape out of the baked piece. These edges can get hard and a bit crusty when baked and it won't matter as it will be discarded. While there is some waste – it is minimal and you can ensure exact shapes and sizes.
Be sure to cut your shape while the bread is still hot/warm. Allow it to cool in the tray before removing.

HELPFUL HINTS

Always line your baking tray with baking paper. There is nothing worse that gingerbread sticking to your baking tray and breaking!

Never leave too much baking paper sticking up at the sides of the tray – trim this down, if they are too large they trap heat and overcook/burn the edges of your bread.

When rolling the gingerbread dough into the baking tray place small, kneaded flattened balls of dough down on the tray – flattening with your fingers as you go and cover half to two thirds of the tray then use your rolling pin to smooth out the base. The gingerbread will stretch and move into place to cover the entire tray evenly.

If you follow this advice and the baking paper keeps sliding about making it difficult – start in the middle of the gingerbread you have placed on the tray with your hands and work back and forth from there with a rolling pin – it provides better control.

If you use a cutter to cut out shapes after you have baked your gingerbread, lightly oil your cutters before you begin. This will reduce any cracks or breaks in the gingerbread as you cut.

OVEN TEMPERATURES

Get to know your oven. Each oven is slightly different and requires adjustment. Don't think because your oven is old it won't be as good, sometimes older ovens bake the best!

Some ovens are fast and some are slow, this means some don't get as hot as the temperature gauge says and some get more so. If you want to get technical you can buy a temperature gauge that goes inside of your oven and you can use that to regulate the temperature. However, I find that despite the temperature gauge, each oven regulates and conducts heat differently and you need to get to know it, like it has its own personality! Be patient, check your gingerbread and don't be alarmed if you're cooking time varies from the recipe, just make a note for next time.

The science of baking is simply the ratio of ingredients and the conditions in which you bake it. The art of baking is knowing how your oven performs and what needs to be changed if anything, to bake evenly.

CONSTRUCTION

Order of construction

It is always best to construct the sides of your gingerbread house first (attaching them to the base piece if there is one), allowing the royal icing to set before adding on any other elements, such as a roof or another story. Allowing this to set provides a sturdy base and helps reduce the risk of breakages or pieces slipping off.

Once you are ready to attach the roof, use royal icing to keep it steady. It should stay in place with the right amount of royal icing however large, thick or severely angled rooves may be pulled down by the their own weight before the royal icing has time to dry and secure them in place. If this happens don't panic – find something in your kitchen (or use gingerbread offcuts) that is the right height to wedge underneath the roof and leave it there until the royal icing dries.

Decorate your display board to create 'the ground' around your house last, as any movement that is made during the house construction, for example, with a collapsed or sliding roof or wall; crumbs from the constructions pieces moving or removal of wedges will get stuck in your wet royal icing or chocolate and ruin your beautiful ground-work.

Reinforced construction

If you have baked quite a soft gingerbread or you are worried about your load bearing pieces in gingerbread house construction you can reinforce the backside of the walls with melted chocolate, this doesn't have to be an embarrassing, unsightly addition. I like to include flavor and color into my reinforcements and make it look like it was part of the design all along. You can use toffee, royal icing or chocolate bark (see page 18) to do this.

SURFACES

Snow-covered surfaces

A snow-covered surface really finishes off your gingerbread house and helps create the whimsical winter scape, an awesome way to complete your overall look. To get a snow covered board you can apply your royal icing two ways:

1. Use a little cranked handled spatula to apply and smooth the royal icing onto the board, making patterns in the snow as you go to give the effect of snow drift.
2. Fill a piping bag with royal icing and using a large round tip (such as a 1A or similar) pipe the snow in lines and swirls to give the effect of snow banks/shovelled snow.

You can also use white chocolate rather than royal icing on the ground surface of your gingerbread house. Be careful as chocolate is temperature sensitive, too hot and it will run right off the board! The best way to do this is to melt a small amount of chocolate at a time and have it at a thick paste consistency (like Nutella), pipe or smooth it into place with a spatula quickly and repeat the process straight away so that the chocolate melts together evenly on the base.

Add an extra element and make your snow look as though it is covered in a layer of little ice crystals! Do this by sprinkling a small amount of white sugar crystals over the top of your royal icing while it is wet – the royal icing will hold it in place and the sugar will sit on the top. Because it is the same color it will blend in giving a hint of texture and catching the light every so often to give off the effect of ice crystals. Otherwise you can dust icing (confectioners) sugar over the surface of dried royal icing to make it look like freshly fallen powder snow.

COLORING FONDANT

Using a fist-sized amount of fondant (or less), knead the fondant with your hands until it 'warms up', making it more pliable.

Then, roll it into a ball and make a well in the center. Add one to two drops of gel food color at a time and close over the well, carefully kneading the ball, folding over the fondant to contain any food color that has not yet been kneaded in. Repeat this until the color starts to become a visible part of the fondant.

Then, take the ball between your palms and roll it into a sausage shape, folding it back on itself and repeating this action until the color is mixed through and looks streaky. The rolling action takes a lot less muscle work than kneading.

Finish mixing the color through evenly by kneading on the bench. If you require a darker color add a few extra drops to the fondant at the streaky phase and repeat the process until you have the desired color. If the fondant feels very soft, do not add icing (confectioners') sugar yet. Instead, wrap it in cling film (plastic wrap) and allow it to sit for half an hour to cool down. After you have let it settle, check to see if it is still very soft and unworkable. If so, add some pure icing sugar to it to make it more workable.

> **TIP:** Creating black or red colored fondant can often prove impossible. It is best to simply purchase black or red fondant from your local cake decorating supply store.

FOOD COLORING

For baking and decorating I use gel or paste food coloring. The color from this product is intense so you don't need much of it. Even though gel and paste food colors are water-based, it is in a concentrated form and the small quantity that you need to add to the fondant or gum paste to get a dramatic color effect will not affect the texture or consistency.

The only exception to this rule is royal icing. You can add a 2 small drops of gel food coloring to royal icing to color it, however if you want to achieve a deep color that requires more dye you may reduce the consistency of the icing, in this instance you may need to add more egg white and icing sugar. For deeper or darker colors, consider reaching the desired shade by color layering rather than sheer volume i.e. to get red, dye the icing orange first.

TEXTURED FONDANT

To create a nicely textured fondant roll out the fondant to the desired thickness on a non-stick surface. Place a clean and dry textured mat over the fondant and rub with the heel of your hand for a light effect, or roll over it with your rolling pin for a deep, more obvious effect.

SILICON MOLDS

Silicon molds, they are so quick, easy and super effective. You can use either gum paste or fondant in your silicon mold, though gum paste is less likely to get stuck!

Before you work with any gum paste in the mold, it's best to put a light coating of cornflour over the mold. This will ensure that your gum paste can be removed easily. If the mold is deeper and more finely detailed, use a heavier coat of cornflour. If it is still difficult to remove, put the full mold into the freezer for 3 minutes, then remove the gum paste shape frozen from the mold. Leave the frozen gum paste to defrost on a non-stick surface before affixing to any gingerbread.

Alternatively, you can spray the silicon mold with a clear vegetable oil release spray. Using this option will leave the figure with an oily sheen. If this is not a desirable look, wait until the gum paste dries hard and brush the surface with cornflour. The cornflour will remove the oily residue and not affect your color or the over all look of your shape.

TURNING FONDANT INTO GUM PASTE

In simplified terms, the key recipe difference between fondant and gum paste is that fondant contains glycerine. Glycerine allows fondant to form a 'crust' or 'skin' on its surface that sets hard enough to the touch on the surface, but underneath the skin, the fondant remains very soft. The removal of glycerine from the formula creates a product that is stiffer to work with and that will dry completely hard given enough time and air.

To save money you can turn fondant into gum paste by adding a CMC (Carboxyl Methyl Cellulose) powder to it. The powder I use starts at a ratio of 1 teaspoon to 250 g (8¾ oz) of fondant. Whether it is fondant or gum paste, make sure it is always wrapped in cling film and air tight to avoid it drying out.

EXTRA ELEMENTS

Adding edible images and fondant windows

To add edible images and fondant to your gingerbread house, follow these simple steps.

1. First, remove your edible image from its backing sheet and cut it into size using scissors or a sharp craft or paring knife. Then place the image cut out onto a piece of thinly rolled out fondant and attach the two with sugar glue.

2. Cut away the excess fondant and allow it to harden slightly on a non-stick surface, or baking paper. Cover the surface with a thin layer of cornflour before leaving to harden to make sure it won't stick. Once the fondant has stiffened slightly, it will be easier to handle and also hold its shape better.

3. Apply a small line of royal icing around the edge of the image and gently lift the image into place, pressing down on the edges of the images slightly to secure the royal icing and help secure it in place.

> **TIP:** The size of your edible image should be the same size as your open window space PLUS an additional edge (called salvage) that will attach the entire shape to the back of the gingerbread.

To make the blinds: Cut a rectangle of fondant and allow it to sit for 1–2 minutes until it become a little stiff in the air but not so dry that it cracks/wrinkles when you work with it.

For roman blinds that look like they fold upwards, fold the fondant from top to bottom like a concertina fan, making large, square folds. Trim off the excess and allow it to dry a little more before securing it in place.

For drapes, cut two rectangles and fold them left to right in a concertina fashion – once folded up, hold the top and let the bottom swing free – work the bottom with your fingers so the curtain looks more open and place onto your gingerbread piece.

To attach blinds to the windows is the same process as attaching the edible images above. When attaching the blind, first use a thin layer of royal icing in the edges of your design as you attach the piece, then go over the blind once attached with a thicker line of royal icing to really secure it.

If you are combining blinds with images, once you have attached the blinds you can simply affix the image or colored fondant directly over the back of the blinds.

PIPING

When piping with royal icing, fill the piping bag to only ⅓ of the bag's volume. This allows the bag to sit in the palm of your hand to give you better control over the movement of the tip and continuity of pressure.

To fill the piping bag, wipe your spatula (or spoon) full of royal icing against the inside of the piping bag, as far down as you can go. When you have filled the bag to the desired level close the sides of the piping bag over from the bottom upwards, this helps to prevent air from being trapped in the bag.

Always twist your piping bag closed at the top and apply pressure from this point to squeeze out the icing at the tip. Squeezing halfway down the bag will only cause the icing to travel up the bag as well as down towards to the tip and result in a mess.

Piping Flood Work

When you choose the design you are going to pipe, have it drawn or printed out in front of you when you start your work so you can keep it as a reference point.

Where possible, have all of the piping bags you will needs ready to use, this will make things quicker and easier for you. To prevent the icing in the tip from drying out, keep the tip end of all of your piping bags wrapped in a (new) damp cloth when they are not in use.

You will need to use a stiff consistency and a finer tip to pipe the border of your shape. Do this for all of your shapes and allow this to dry before continuing with the flood work.

Next, add a little more liquid to your white and colored royal icing and pipe this within the border of your shape within the corresponding color, the more fluid nature of this mix means it should bleed out into this space filling it up without lines. Be careful not to overfill it as you just want to fill the crevasse to the point that the fluid mixture beads over the edge of the stiff border. I use a rounded piping tip at least a size #3, larger if you have a bigger area to fill.

ONLAY MOLDS

Onlay molds are silicon molds that allow you to create even, neat, fondant overlays They are great for creating a roof (see page 71 for the Russian Doll House and page 47 for the Cuckoo Clock).

To use an onlay mold, dust it with cornflour and then remove this later once the pattern is in place by brushing it gently with Cake Decorator's Rose Spirit. Dusting your mold is optional.

Next, roll out your fondant on a non-stick surface making sure it is not too thick. Place your rolled fondant over the top of your onlay mold and using your rolling pin, gently roll over the top of your fondant so that sinks into the mold and any raised sections of the mold are exposed and clearly visible. If your mold requires it, use a Dresden tool or toothpick to remove any shapes that do not belong in your pattern.

Next, place a small amount of sugar glue to the fondant still in the onlay mold, this will adhere it to the fondant on the gingerbread. If you are placing the onlay pattern directly onto gingerbread you will need to use piping gel or a small amount of royal icing for the mold to stick.

Once you have a layer of glue on the fondant in the mold, lift the mold into place over the gingerbread panel and place it face down. This glue side has now become the back of your onlay design and will stick.

To remove the silicon mold start at one end and gently peel the mold backwards ensuring the fondant has let go of the mold at both sides before peeling back, if it has stuck gently use your finger or Dresden tool to loosen it.

CAKE LACE

To use a silicon lace matt, fist make sure it is clean and dry and on a flat surface.

Make up your cake lace according to the manufacturer's instructions. To apply the cake lace, use a crank handled spatula at a 45° angle and working from one side to the other, scrape the cake lace mixture into the mat. Depending on which brand you use, the mix will need to be either oven-baked or left overnight to set.

To remove the cake lace, place the mat face down onto a sheet of baking paper. Bend back one end of the mat and gently loosen the lace. To cut cake lace to size use a heavy-handled knife or embroidery scissors.

To affix the cake lace, use clear sugar glue or piping gel to stick it to the gingerbread or fondant.

The Button House

Sweet and simple, this house is perfect for beginners, or to make in an afternoon with kids.

TO MAKE THIS YOU'LL NEED:

1 x display board

Royal icing

Sprinkles

Silicon button molds

Colored fondant (or white fondant and gel food color) in the following colors; forest green, sky blue, lemon yellow, red, orange

Cornflour (for dusting)

125g (4oz) melting chocolate

paring knife

Large piping tip or spatula (to apply royal icing to the board)

Small piping tip (to apply royal icing to back of buttons)

METHOD:

1. To make the gingerbread, follow the gingerbread recipe of your choice from the gingerbread chapter (page 8).

2. If you have not pre-cut your shapes before baking, use your templates to cut the shapes out of your fresh baked gingerbread using a small paring knife. Allow the gingerbread to cool and transfer to a wire rack to come to room temperature and stiffen a little. You can leave it over night for maximum durability. Create templates for the dimensions (below) on A4 paper. Refer to page 116 for templates. Cut the paper to the following dimensions:

- Front and back panel (make 2): 10cm wide x 13cm tall (3.9in x 5in), with triangular roof section at top.
- Sides (make 2): 9cm wide x 7cm tall (3.5in x 2.7in)
- Roof (make 2): 13.5cm wide x 10cm tall (5.3in x 3.9in)

3. Cut the gingerbread to fit the template and stick the pieces together using the royal icing.

4. While the gingerbread dries, make the buttons using ready-to-roll fondant. To do this, lightly dust your button mold with cornflour, tapping out the excess. Knead a small ball of fondant between your fingers and place it into the mold, using your fingers work it into the mold so it fills any open spaces.

5. Turn the mold upside down onto a flat, non-stick surface and peel the mold back using your finger to gently coax out any stubborn buttons. Make as many buttons as you require for your design. You can dust off any excess cornflour left on the face of your buttons using Cake Decorator's Rose Spirit or clear alcohol. Paint the buttons will the food coloring of your choice to create colorful buttons. Set aside to dry.

6. If you prefer to make your buttons from chocolate; melt the chocolate as per the packet instructions. Once melted, add in the color if desired and pour the chocolate into the silicone button mold and leave to set.

7. Once set, remove the chocolate buttons and set aside.

8. Put the remaining Royal icing into a into a piping bag and, using a small tip, squeeze the icing on the back of the buttons and secure the buttons onto the roof, sides and front of the house. You can apply the buttons to the roof in any pattern you like.

9. Once this is done, cover the cake board with royal icing. Sprinkle the royal icing with multi-colored sprinkles before it dries completely.

Variations: To decorate the house, decorate with whatever candies and chocolate you prefer. You can also pipe royal icing to create decorative designs around the walls of the house and roof.

The Church

A classic gingerbread church house that can be adapted to suit any celebration.

TO MAKE THIS YOU'LL NEED:

1 x display board

Royal icing

Wood grain texture mat

Fondant/gum paste (for edible image and door)

Edible image (2 different kinds) of stained glass pattern

Brown fondant (or white fondant and brown gel food color)

Sugar glue

Paring knife

Rolling pin

METHOD:

1. To make the gingerbread, follow the gingerbread recipe of your choice from the gingerbread chapter (page 8).

2. If you have not pre-cut your shapes before baking, use your templates to cut the shapes out of your fresh baked gingerbread using a small paring knife. Allow the gingerbread to cool and transfer to a wire rack to come to room temperature and stiffen a little. You can leave it over night for maximum durability. Create templates for the dimensions (below) on A4 paper. Refer to page 118 for templates. Cut the paper to the following dimensions:

- Front and back panel (make 2): 14cm wide x 24cm tall (5.5in x 9.4in) with triangular roof section at top – use a proportionately sized circle cutter to remove a circle from the top ⅓ of the front panel and a square/arch cutter or template for the door. Do this for both front and back panels in case one is damaged.
- Sides (make 2): 17cm wide x 12cm tall (6.7in x 4.7in) using an arch cutter or template remove arch shapes for side windows.
- Roof (make 2): 19cm wide x 14cm tall (7.4in x 5.5in)

3. Prepare the royal icing in a piping bag and use the icing to stick the gingerbread pieces together. Set aside to dry.

4. Before constructing your sides you need to add your stain glass windows. First remove your edible image from its backing sheet and cut it into size using scissors or a sharp paring knife. Then place the image cut out onto a piece of thinly rolled out fondant and attach the two with sugar glue.

5. Cut away the excess fondant and allow it to harden slightly on a non-stick surface. Cover the surface with a thin layer of cornflour before leaving to harden to avoid it sticking.

6. Apply a small line of royal icing around the edge of the image and gently lift the image into place, pressing down on the edges of the images to slightly sqash the royal icing and help secure it in place.

7. Assemble your gingerbread house using royal icing, starting with the sides, allowing them to dry completely before attaching the roof.

8. To create the brown colored fondant floor, roll out the fondant to a size only slightly larger than your floor space, so that when you construct the church, the sides sit on top of the fondant. (See page 26 for more on adding a texture to the fondant.)

9. To create the door, take the square of gingerbread that was cut out of the front panel and affix wood textured brown fondant over it with a small amount of royal icing, then texture it to look like wood and secured back onto the final structure to look like a welcoming open door.

> **TIP:** If you want add depth of color or extra interest to your floors or door you can use an edible petal dust or gel food coloring mixed with Cake Decorator's Rose Spirit and paint over the textured wood/brick surface – the color will collect and concentrate in the crevasses of the embossed area and make it look darker in these spots adding dimension to your work.

The Beach House

TIME

DIFFICULTY

If you are having Christmas in a hot climate like Australia – why not make your gingerbread house representative of the weather and all the things we love about Christmas down under – the beach!

TO MAKE THIS YOU'LL NEED:

Rolling pin

Sugar glue

Royal icing

125g (4oz) melting chocolate

Silicon molds or cutters (for leaves and flowers)

Edible image for windows

Gum paste (for curtains)

Ruler

Paring knife

White fondant tinted; grey (using black dye), orange, yellow (for sand), green (light and dark), brown, blue

Edible silver paint (optional)

Two display boards (1 large and 1 small)

Brick texture mat

233 grass tip

Square cutters or template (for windows)

Rectangle cutters or template (for solar panels)

White sugar (for sand)

Spatula (for sand)

- Front panel with windows: 11cm wide x 15cm tall (4.3in x 5.9in) *
- Front panel without windows: 9cm wide x 15cm tall (3.5in x 5.9in)
- Back panel: 20cm wide x 21cm tall (7.9in x 8.3in) with triangular roof section at top
- Long side: 25cm x 15cm tall (9.8in x 5.9in)
- Short side: 18cm wide x 15cm tall (7in x 5.9in)
- Door panel: 7cm wide x 15cm tall (2.8in x 5.9in)
- Roof panel (make 2): 28cm wide x 13cm tall (11in x 5.1in)
- Roof triangle panel: 20cm wide x 6cm tall (7.9in x 2.3in)

> **TIP:** *To make one of these panels with windows when the piece comes out of the oven, remove four squares to make a window on both the left and right side.

METHOD:

1. To make the gingerbread, follow the gingerbread recipe of your choice from the gingerbread chapter (page 8).

2. If you have not pre-cut your shapes before baking, use your templates to cut the shapes out of your fresh baked gingerbread using a small paring knife. Allow the gingerbread to cool and transfer to a wire rack to come to room temperature and stiffen a little. You can leave it over night for maximum durability. Create templates for the dimensions (below) on A4 paper. Refer to page 120 for templates. Cut the paper to the following dimensions:

3. Once the gingerbread is cooked, prepare the royal icing in a piping bag and use the icing to stick the gingerbread pieces together. Set aside to dry.

4. Once cool, you can assemble your gingerbread house using royal icing, starting with the sides, allowing them to dry completely before attaching the roof pieces. If you are adding stain glass windows and curtains, make sure you attach these before you start construction. (See page 28 for how to affix edible images and make curtains.)

5. To create the decking roll out and cut the dark brown fondant to size and texture with wood grain (see page 26 for more on textured fondant). Then, layer over the edge of the smaller board onto the larger board. Once layered,

imprint the fondant with a metal ruler to create the illusion of a two-tier deck.

6. Next, create the path outside the house. Use the lighter brown fondant, textured with a brick texture mat to create a brick-like effect. Once textured, add the fondant around the side of the board in a path shape.

7. To create the concrete slab at the front door, roll the grey fondant out into small balls and press them down on the board, creating a cobblestoned look.

8. Next, using a 233 grass tip, pipe the green colored royal icing around the front and sides of the beach house to create the grass.

9. The addition of sand down one side is optional. To make it, combine castor sugar and yellow food coloring and then add white royal icing to make a yellow, granular paste. The Royal icing will take on the color of the sugar. Apply to the board with a small spatula or your fingers for greater control.

10. The leaves and flower decorations were made using a silicon mold (see page 27) and attached using a small amount of royal icing.

11. To make the fondant surfboards, first create a template by folding a small piece of paper in half and drawing one half of the surfboard. Leaving the paper folded, cut out the shape to get your surfboard template.

12. Next, roll out your gum paste on a non stick surface and using a paring knife, cut around your template. Once you have cut out the surfboards, leave them to dry pointy end up. When your surfboards are hardened you can add designs of your choice using edible food color, pens or images.

13. To create the solar panels, roll out a thin square of grey gum paste and allow it to dry before adding 8 long rectangles of thick fondant on top using sugar glue. You can create a texture on the fondant using a brand new scouring pad or impression mat. Once your solar panel is dried hard you can affix it to the roof using royal icing, propping up the top part with two small balls of fondant for an authentic look.

14. Next, make the roof tiles. To create the tile color I have used, mix brown and orange food dye in with the fondant. Roll out the fondant and cut it into small (2cm x 2cm / 0.8in

x 0.8in) squares. Then layer the squares over the roof joint at the top of the house and securing in place with with royal icing.

15. To fill in the triangles underneath the roof at the front and back of the house, roll out some grey fondant and cut it to size (you can use the template to do this). Use a thin metal ruler to create thin indents horizontally down the fondant to create a wooden look and attach with a small amount of royal icing.

16. To create the sliding door, roll out your blue fondant very thin and cut out a large rectnagle shape. Next using a clay extruder or ruler cut out 5 long thin rectangle shapes to make the borders of the door. Affix to the blue fondant with sugar glue. Paint the borders with edible silver paint for a metallic look. Affix the shape to the house with royal icing.

17. To create the pot plants at the back door, use your fingers to mold two small balls and use your ball tool to create a depression in the top. Add on a small amount of brown fondant, and add three small leaves from green fondant to add on top.

18. Lastly, make the bougainvillea. Here I have used a

silicon mold for the vines and flowers (see page 27). Affix the vines to the house using royal icing.

Note: This house has been constructed on a small board that was then attached to a larger display board, to give the illusion of landscaping. To attach boards simply use royal icing, melted chocolate or hot glue.

TIP: Assemble the front panel of the house and front door first – that way if you are slightly off it won't be obvious.

The Bird House

Bird houses are so quaint and delicate, usually seen on the front pretty Christmas cards all covered in snow, the humble bird house is making a comeback and not just for Christmas.!

TO MAKE THIS YOU'LL NEED:

6 gingerbread pieces

Fondant in baby pink and baby blue or white fondant and soft pink and corn flower blue gel food coloring

White gum paste or tylose to place into your white fondant to turn it into gum paste

Texture mat 'handbag' or 'chain' pattern (for roof fondant)

Medium sized blossom cutter

Extra small blossom cutter – plunger or cutter and small ball tool

Silicon mold for a 2D bird

Circle cutter

Display board

Embossing tools (I have used Wilton embossing set)

Sugar glue

Royal icing

Lollies for the center (optional)

Rolling pin

METHOD:

1. To make the gingerbread, follow the gingerbread recipe of your choice from the gingerbread chapter (page 8).

2. If you have not pre-cut your shapes before baking, use your templates to cut the shapes out of your fresh baked gingerbread using a small paring knife. Allow the gingerbread to cool and transfer to a wire rack to come to room temperature and stiffen a little. You can leave it over night for maximum durability. Create templates for the dimensions (below) on A4 paper. Refer to page 124 for templates. Cut the paper to the following dimensions:

- Front and back panel (make 2): 7cm wide x 20cm tall (2.7in x 7.8in)
- Sides (make 2): 7cm wide x 8.5cm tall (2.7in x 3.3in)
- Roof (make 2): 15.5cm wide x 7.5cm tall (6in x 2.9in)

3. Apply your fondant coverings to the gingerbread pieces before constructing the house.

4. Start with the roof by rolling out your pink fondant, emboss it using your texture mat and apply to the roof piece with royal icing.

5. Next, cover the side and front pieces in pale blue fondant. To create the ornate detail, use a Wilton embossing tool immediately after applying and trimming the blue fondant to fit the piece. Pipe over this detail with royal icing or leave embossed. Remember: a little says a lot – I have left the embossed patterns rather than piping over them because the white of the tree branches with piping as well would mean the front would look too busy – keep a nice contrast to create interest and avoid it looking messy.

6. To create the tree branches, roll out some white fondant between your palms to create long, thin sausages, then cut to length and bend and twist them to suit your design. Affix them in place using sugar glue.

7. Next, create little violet flowers to add onto the branches. For this design I used a very small blossom ejector cutter that pushed in the center of the flowers giving their petals a slight curl upwards. If you are using a standard cutter you can push a small ball tool onto the center of the flower after cutting it out to give the petals the same curl at the edges. Secure them in place with sugar glue or royal icing depending on their weight. If you choose to make little curled roses or heavier flowers, avoid disappointment and secure them in place with royal icing to be sure they will not falloff and break.

8. To make the bird use white gum paste in a silicon mold and secure the bird to the house using royal icing. It is best to make the bird early and allow it to dry hard before attaching to the final house structure, this will help it to sit upright.

9. Construct the house laying down by first attaching

the sides to the back panel, support the side pieces with household items of appropriate size. Once this is dry, sit the house upright and attach the front panel with royal icing and allow this to dry. Once dry add the roof pieces.

10. Next, use a medium-sized blossom cutter to cut flower shapes out of white fondant to add to the edges of the gingerbread roof.

> **TIP:** Use an appropriately proportionate sized circle cutter to remove a circle from the top third of the front panel. Do this for both front and back panels in case one is damaged—use the best one and put the lesser of the two as the back panel, plugging the hole with the removed circle biscuit.

Cuckoo clock

My fascination with cuckoo clocks most certainly arises from the love I have for the film *The Sound of Music*. There is something romantically European about the cuckoo clock sounding its chimes around Christmas. Nowhere near as ornate and detailed as some of the other houses, but cute as anything!

TO MAKE THIS YOU'LL NEED:

Fondant; chocolate brown, green, red, ivory or white fondant and gel food coloring

2 acorns – I have used porcelain Christmas ornaments that formed part of the gift

Plastic figurines: reindeer, mushroom and tree

Onlay mold in shell pattern (for roof)

Small sized ivy cutter

Heart cutter

Display board

Silicon mold for a 3D bird, a fake bird (like a Christmas decoration) or a bird modelled from gum paste and painted.

Circle cutter

Metal ruler to emboss lines or Embossing tool

Sugar glue

Royal icing

Lollies for the center (optional)

Rolling pin

Edible gold paint

Silicon mold of a Christmas wreath

Edible image of a clock face (you can use paper as long as this part is not consumed)

Texture mat of snowflakes for the board

METHOD:

1. To make the gingerbread, follow the gingerbread recipe of your choice from the gingerbread chapter (page 8).

2. If you have not pre-cut your shapes before baking, use your templates to cut the shapes out of your fresh baked gingerbread using a small paring knife. Allow the gingerbread to cool and transfer to a wire rack to come to room temperature and stiffen a little. You can leave it over night for maximum durability. See page 126 for dimensions.

3. Start by covering your display board with red fondant. (See page 26 for how to best use a texture mat.)

4. Once the gingerbread is cooked, before assembling cover each piece of gingerbread with fondant.

5. To decorate the front of the cuckoo clock, cover it with ivory fondant and use a metal ruler to imprint lines at equal spaces apart. This gives a wood panel effect. Do the same for the clock base (pointy end).

6. Next, roll out the chocolate colored fondant to create sausage shapes. Place them onto the clock face and bend and twist them to create tree branches. Once you are happy with the style and positioning – stick in place with sugar glue.

7. Add the red fondant hearts to the end of each branch.

8. Then add on the onlay mold shell pattern onto the roof pieces using sugar glue or piping gel.

9. Once this is done, prepare the royal icing in a piping bag and use the icing to cover the 'shelf' piece of gingerbread. While the royal icing is wet, affix your little plastic figurines in place. Set aside to dry.

10. Only when the royal icing is hard and the embellishments secured can you assemble the clock.

11. Assemble the clock in three stages: clock, shelf, then base – waiting for each part to dry before adding the next.

12. Add ivy or seasonal leaves to the border of your clock to add detail and interest. I have used a small ivy ejector cutter that embosses the leaves and affixed with royal icing.

13. Then use a silicon mold (see page 27) or holly leaf

cutters and arrange them into a wreath. Add little red berries (small rolled up pieces of red fondant) to add dimension to the wreath. Once dry, paint the bow on the wreath with edible gold paint.

14. Next, make the clock face. Roll out the remaining fondant quite thick and cut out a circle. Once the fondant dries, paint over it with edible gold paint and stick the clock face image over the top.

15. Once the clock face is dry affix it to your clock with royal icing.

16. To attach the base of the clock you need two pieces of gingerbread to act like pylons under a bridge. Secure them in place with royal icing and allow them to dry completely before sticking your clock base to both them and the underside of the shelf. Ensure all decorating has been completed before attaching this piece to avoid breakages and disappointment.

17. For this design I have used porcelain acorn ornaments and positioned those both close up under the base of the clock – while this is not technically correct positioning space did not allow for one to be longer than the other so I have improvised. You can easily make acorns with fondant or gum paste, both with or without foam ball centers however using a foam ball center for gum paste figures of this size will help drying and prevent breakages. You may wish to use real acorns or pine cones – if so be sure to wash and dry them thoroughly and don't allow them to touch the edible parts of the clock. However you choose to make the weights for your cuckoo clock – secure them in place with royal icing.

18. This bird was made in advance using a three stage process including fondant, gum paste and edible paint. Making this requires advanced skills that require a tutorial you can find on line, otherwise you can buy 3D silicon molds to make the bird, use a beautifully crafted, light Christmas ornament or even make it 2D using an edible image on gum paste (see 3D Reindeer on page 91).

Note: Due to the size of this structure you may need to place supports inside the house while the walls dry, like a can of soup or empty mug.

TIP: Use an appropriately proportionate sized circle cutter to remove a circle from the front panel. Do this for both front and back panels in case one is damaged – use the best one and put the lesser of the two as the back panel, plugging the hole with the removed circle biscuit.

Modern Candy House

Want to make a super simple, easy gingerbread house? Try this modern take on the classic gingerbread house. Complete with lollipops, gumballs and chocolate freckles. This house is a really easy one to adapt to suit the dimensions of your own home.

TO MAKE THIS YOU'LL NEED:

9 piece gingerbread + the door

Royal icing

Tip and piping bag

Display board

Gumballs

Lollipops

Freckle chocolates

Sherbet brick lollies / lollies (for front path)

Fondant (blue)

Rolling pin

METHOD:

1. To make the gingerbread, follow the gingerbread recipe of your choice from the gingerbread chapter (page 8).

2. If you have not pre-cut your shapes before baking, use your templates to cut the shapes out of your fresh baked gingerbread using a small paring knife. Allow the gingerbread to cool and transfer to a wire rack to come to room temperature and stiffen a little. You can leave it over night for maximum durability. Create templates for the dimensions (below) on A4 paper. Refer to page 128 for templates. Cut the paper to the following dimensions:

Angled side of the house

- Roof (make 1): 16cm wide x 14cm tall (6.2in x 5.5in)
- Front and back panel (make 2): 17.5cm wide (12.5cm on shorter end) x 13cm tall (6.8in high (4.9in on shorter end) x 5in tall)
- Side panel – short (make 1): 14cm wide x 12.5cm tall (5.5in x 6.8in)
- Side panel – tall (make 1): 17.5cm wide x 13cm tall (6.8in x 5in)

Square side of the house

- Roof (make 1): 15cm wide x 14cm tall (5.9in x 5.5in)
- Front and back panel (make 2): 15cm wide x 13cm tall (5.9in x 5in)
- Side panel (make 1): 15cm wide x 14cm tall (5.9in x 5.5in)
- Door (make 1): proportional to the size of your windows

3. Construct the walls of your angled side first, allow it to dry a little and construct the square side onto the angled side. You will not need a second side panel for the square part of the house because will fit directly onto the side panel of the sloped side of the house. Allow the royal icing for both to set hard before adding the roofs.

4. Attach both roof pieces with royal icing and allow to dry before adding the chocolate freckles along the top of the roof. Apply a small amount of royal icing or melted chocolate to the back of the freckles to secure them in place.

5. Next, make the path. Using sherbet bricks as your pavers, apply a small amount of royal icing to the board and place your pavers on top.

6. Add the door using royal icing. Pipe a single dot for the door handle.

7. Cover the board with royal icing using a spatula in a swirling motion. Do this in sections so you can maximize the decoration of your board. I.e. the front left section of the house, the front right section of the house, down the right side of the house, across the back then up the left side of the house.

8. To secure the lollipop topiary trees, apply a small amount of royal icing to the side of the lollipop that will touch the side of the house. Insert them into the royal-iced

board and get them to hold themselves up by the royal icing affixing them to the side of the house.

9. To make the low shrubs that border the ginger property – position brightly colored gumballs in a straight line. Have fun with your color matching.

10. Fondant windows have been done by simply rolling out blue fondant and cutting it into shape free hand using a paring knife. If you are unsure, make paper templates, check them against your gingerbread pieces or template and use them to cut out your blue fondant.

11. Affix your blue fondant to the front of your house with a small amount of royal icing – pipe around the fondant shape.

12. To decorate the house, decorate with whatever candies and chocolate you prefer. You can also pipe royal icing to create decorative designs around the walls of the house and roof – the limit is your imagination.

> **TIP:** To maximize neatness in your piping – apply the windows and pipe around them before constructing. This makes it a tad more difficult to line the windows up – so lay your two front panel pieces side by side, with the base of each piece in a straight line, then position your fondant – this way you can see how they will look standing up side by side.

Caravan

Holidaying around in a Caravan is a classic summer pastime for many families. So, why not celebrate in style with a caravan gingerbread house!

I have gone retro with my shapes and colors in this design because it's just so iconic. Adapt the template, colors and trimmings using the skills outlined in this book to make it your own.

TO MAKE THIS, YOU'LL NEED:

Rolling pin

Sugar glue

Silicon mold for tyres

Display board

Fondant (for door, window, curtains, steps, brick, towbar and tyres)

Black fondant

White fondant tinted; Maroon, Ivory, Navy, Sky Blue and Green (for grass)

Edible silver paint

Ruler

Paring knife

233 grass tip

Piping bag

Template (for windows and door)

Royal icing

Large and small rounded piping tip

METHOD:

1. To make the gingerbread, follow the gingerbread recipe of your choice from the gingerbread chapter (page 8).

2. When creating templates for the dimensions on A4 paper remember, depth can be varied easily while still using all of these measurements but be careful not to go too wide, especially if you are scaling down the dimensions of a real caravan to make a replica. Make a paper template of your replica and put it all together to be sure it still looks in proportion.

3. If you have not pre-cut your shapes before baking, use your templates to cut the shapes out of your fresh baked gingerbread using a small paring knife. Allow the gingerbread to cool and transfer to a wire rack to come to room temperature and stiffen a little. You can leave it over night for maximum durability. Create templates for the dimensions (below) on A4 paper. Refer to page 130 for templates. Cut the paper to the following dimensions:

- Front and back (make 2): 14cm wide x 16cm tall (5.5in x 6.3in) – this reaches 20cm wide at center, refer to templates for complete dimensions
- Base side panels (make 2): 5cm wide x 6cm tall (2in x 2.4in)
- Left side panel: 5cm wide x 10cm tall (2in x 3.9in)
- Right side panel 1: 5cm wide x 8cm tall (2in x 3.1in)
- Right side panel 2: 5cm wide x 2 cm tall (2in x 0.8in)

4. Assemble your gingerbread house using royal icing, starting with the back, roof and sides, allowing them to dry for attaching the front panel. It is best to construct this piece laying flat and sit it upright when it is dry. To make the windows, door and iconic retro colors strips down the side use thinly rolled out fondant and affix it in place using royal icing.

5. Make the navy blind on the side window by folding a rectangle of fondant in a concertina fashion and affixing it in place with royal icing. The addition of a small roll of white fondant to sit over the top of it – painted in edible silver paint lends authenticity as a housing unit and balances out the design. You can use silver paint accents to represent the metal framing of caravans and the cover some of the exposed gingerbread.

6. Next, make the tyres using black fondant and, a small tyre mold (see page 27 for more on using silicon molds).

7. To create the steps, cut out 3 rectangles of thickly rolled out fondant, and allow them to dry. Then stack them, using royal icing to glue them together and to the display board (as an anchor point). Paint over the steps with edible silver paint. Use the same method to create the bricks that hold up the tow bar at the back end of the caravan.

8. Make the towbar by rolling one sausage shape with white fondant and bending it like a hairpin, before setting aside to dry hard. Once the fondant is dry, add a ball on top using sugar glue and paint both the hairpin bars and ball silver using edible paint. Once the pieces are dry attach the towbar to the caravan using royal icing.

9. To secure the bricks to the board use a small amount of green royal icing. Cover the edges of this and the rest of the board using the 233 grass tip to pipe luscious green summer grass.

10. Add the silver trim on the window using additional blue fondant. Use a metal ruler to make indented marks into the fondant to create the impression of a frame. When the fondant is dry, paint over the frame with edible silver paint.

TIPS: Decorate the front panel first before assembling to ensure you get everything straight. (It's easier.)

Assemble the caravan flat, start with the back of the van on a flat surface and build the sides, allowing them to dry before adding the front.

Add the front last and allow it to dry before standing it up.

If you are slightly off center don't worry – as long as your van is straight at the top you can cover the bottom with longer grass or tyres positioned lower.

Pink Dollhouse

I just adore triangular dollhouses! Real ones, toy ones and even gingerbread ones! The shape of this house, like many others in the book, lends itself really well to being filled with lollies or other treats as a surprise inside. The great thing about this house is that it only requires you to bake 4 pieces!

TO MAKE THIS YOU'LL NEED:

4 gingerbread pieces

Display board

Fondant in baby pink and or white fondant and soft pink gel food coloring

Edible silver paint

Small sized heart cutter

Silicon mold for an ornate heart

Silicon mold for a bow

Musk sticks

Marshmallows

Gumballs

Mini marshmallow

Sprinkles

Edible pink pearls

Royal icing

Lollies for the center (optional)

Rolling pin

Spatula

Small round piping tip and piping bag is recommended to neatly apply royal icing to the back of the little hearts

Ruler – if you need help applying the hearts to the roof in straight lines

METHOD:

1. To make the gingerbread, follow the gingerbread recipe of your choice from the gingerbread chapter (page 8). You will only need to make 4 large pieces.

2. If you have not pre-cut your shapes before baking, use your templates to cut the shapes out of your fresh baked gingerbread using a small paring knife. Allow the gingerbread to cool and transfer to a wire rack to come to room temperature and stiffen a little. You can leave it over night for maximum durability. Create templates for the dimensions (below) on A4 paper. Refer to page 132 for templates. Cut the paper to the following dimensions:

- Front and back panel of house – triangular (make 2): 20cm wide x 19cm tall (7.8in x 7.4in)
- Roof panels (make 2): 21cm wide x 15cm tall (8.2in x 5.9in) (more if you require additional overhang of the roof)

3. When assembling this make a mark along the board the same depth as the roof and position the front and back panels over the end of these lines with royal icing and leave a drinking glass or other household item behind them to prop them up. Once the royal icing is dry affix the roof panels one at a time using royal icing. Wait for it to dry completely before adding any decoration.

4. To decorate, pre-cut little pink hearts out of fondant using a shape cutter and put them aside to stiffen slightly. Affix them to the roof panels using royal icing in straight lines, painting over a few hearts with edible silver paint for effect.

5. Next, line the edges of the dollhouse with pink musk sticks and affix them into place with royal icing.

6. Create the ornate heart center piece and the cute bow by using silicon molds (see page 27) and affix it to your house with royal icing between the musk sticks.

7. Next, attach a door to the front of the house. First, apply royal icing the top and sides of the door and dip all sides into a small bowl of edible pink pearl sprinkles, then apply more royal icing to the back of the door to affix it to the front of the house.

8. To decorate the 'garden' on the board, cover your

board with royal icing using a spatula one area at a time. I have used musk sticks to line the garden path which is covered in mini marshmallows. The ground around the house has been covered in pink and white heart shaped sprinkles. For the hedges and shrubs i have used pearly pink gum balls and large pink and white marshmallows into the royal icing.

9. To decorate the house, decorate with whatever lollies and chocolate you prefer. You can also pipe royal icing to create decorative designs around the walls of the house and roof.

Note: if you are adding a surprise inside – add one roof panel and use the gap left waiting for the last roof panel as your access point to put the surprise candies etc in. Do not fill it so that there is pressure on the roof or front and back panels as this may cause breakages.

TIPS: To keep it Christmas themed simply change the color scheme to red, green and white and add some Candy Canes to the garden.

Don't want to make a door specifically for this? Try square pink wafer biscuits instead. One directly onto the front panel or if you are going to border it with pink pearls – first stick two wafers together for extra strength to avoid breakages

Small little hearts too fiddly? Don't like working with fondant? Cover the roof the same way but use pre-made love heart lollies that have super cute messages on them. Add a foil covered chocolate heart (with lots of royal icing on the back) for the ornate piece on the front!

The School

Making a gingerbread school is super fun! For this design I chose an old-English style primary school because they are just so quaint and have an old style architecture that makes it immediately recognizable as a school. If you want to make a replica of your school, find a design with a similar shape and adapt it or draw your own template – but remember – proportion is everything!

TO MAKE THIS YOU'LL NEED:

13 pieces of gingerbread + a door

Display board

Royal icing

Large and small round piping tip

White fondant and gel food colors; yellow, orange, brown

Mold for a bell

Edible image for a clock (note you can use paper if you can ensure no one will eat this component)

Edible gold paint

Brick texture mat

Wood texture mat

Crest template

Square cutters small and large/window and door

Round cutter

Rectangle cutter

Sugar glue

METHOD:

1. To make the gingerbread, follow the gingerbread recipe of your choice from the gingerbread chapter (page 8). You will need to make 13 pieces plus enough for a gingerbread door.

2. If you have not pre-cut your shapes before baking, use your templates to cut the shapes out of your fresh baked gingerbread using a small paring knife. Allow the gingerbread to cool and transfer to a wire rack to come to room temperature and stiffen a little. You can leave it over night for maximum durability. Create templates for the dimensions (below) on A4 paper. Refer to page 133 for templates. Cut the paper to the following dimensions

(this design can be viewed and constructed in 4 sections: ground level, right wing and left wing, 2nd story):

Ground floor

- Front and back Panel (make 2): 35cm wide x 10cm tall (13.7in x 3.9in)
- Roof (make 1): 35cm wide x 10cm tall (13.7in x 3.9in)

Right and left wings (same)

- Outer side panel (covers ground floor and outside of wing) (make 2): 26cm wide x 10cm tall (10in x 3.9in)
- Inside panel (covers inside of wing only) (make 2): 16cm wide x 10cm tall (6.2in x 3.9in)
- Front panel (make 2): 10cm wide x 17cm tall (3.9in x 6.7in)
- Roof (make 4): 18cm wide x 9.5cm tall (7in x 3.7in)

2nd Story

- Front and back panel (make 2): 14cm wide x 10cm tall (5.5in x 3.9in)
- Side panels (make 2): 10cm wide x 17cm tall (3.9in x 6.7in)
- Roof (make 2): 14cm wide x 9–9.5cm tall (5.5in x 3.5–3.7in) (with or without overhang)

3. First, construct the windows using fondant windows (see page 28). Once prepared, use a small square and rectangle cutters to remove holes while the shape is still hot from the oven. After allowing it to cool and reinforcing the back of the pieces, the yellow glow of bulb lighting is created by adding a rolled out piece of fondant to the back of the gingerbread pieces.

4. When constructing place the front panel of the ground floor first and then build its sides and backing. Then construct the right and left wings, starting with the longer side panels first, the then shorter inside panel, add the front panel last and allowing it all to dry before adding the roof. Lastly, construct the second story like you would a normal gingerbread house.

5. Once the school is constructed begin decorating.

6. Use a circle cutter to make a round fondant disc slightly larger than the edible image of a clock face. Cut out the image and affix with sugar glue. Affix entire clock face to the front of the school with royal icing.

7. Next, create the bell. For this one i have used a silicon mold (see page 27).

8. To create the door, roll out a small amount of brown fondant and apply a wood grain texture on top of it. Affix the fondant piece to the door using a small amount of royal icing. Attach two small balls to the door for handles and color them with edible gold paint.

9. Next, make the front path using light brown and orange gel color on fondant to create orange-brown brick themed pathway. Create the brick texture using a brickwork texture mat.

10. Lastly, pipe the snow on the ground using a large rounded piping tip (I have used a 1A) and pipe the royal icing onto the board in straight lines. If your royal icing is less stiff than construction consistency the piped lines of royal icing should slightly sink into each other creating a look like they have been freshly shovelled.

Beach Sheds

The classic beach shed is iconic around the world. From the bright Beach sheds of England's Torquay to Australia's Great Ocean Road, beach houses can be found all around the world, including France, South Africa and Sweden! Simple, effective and quick and easy to make – you can choose to cover the entire shed with fondant like I have here or just opt for the bright doors and trim if you like your gingerbread less decorated.

TO MAKE THIS YOU WILL NEED:

6 gingerbread pieces per hut (so 24 have been used here)

White fondant for the hut panels and gel food coloring to color the grey roof and brightly colored doors and eaves. for this i have used: black, sky, blue, lemon yellow, orange, and the red fondant has been purchased pre colored.

Texture mat 'corrugated' or 'ribbed' pattern

Display board

Paring knife

Ruler (metal)

Clay extruder (optional)

Silver edible paint (optional – can use grey fondant)

Royal icing

Rounded piping tip

Piping bag

Rolling pin

Cornflour for dusting

Lollies for the center (optional)

Rectangle cutter

Sugar glue

METHOD:

1. To make the gingerbread, follow the gingerbread recipe of your choice from the gingerbread chapter (page 8). You will need to make 6 pieces per hut.

2. If you have not pre-cut your shapes before baking, use your templates to cut the shapes out of your fresh baked gingerbread using a small paring knife. Allow the gingerbread to cool and transfer to a wire rack to come to room temperature and stiffen a little. You can leave it over night for maximum durability. Create templates for the dimensions (below) on A4 paper. Refer to page 136 for templates. Cut the paper to the following dimensions:

- Front and back panel (make 2 per hut): 8cm wide x 17.5cm tall (3in x 6.8in)
- Side panels (make 2): 6cm wide x 12cm tall (2.3in x 4.7in)
- Roof panels (make 2): 8cm wide x 6.5cm tall (3in x 2.5in)

3. Before construction, cover each panel with fondant. To get the texture in the fondant, roll out your fondant and affix it to the gingerbread piece with royal icing smoothing as you go. Trim where necessary and using a ruler, emboss horizontal lines to give the effect of wood panelling (if desired).

4. Once shapes are decorated, secure them together using royal icing.

5. To make the roof, a small amount of black gel food color into white fondant to create a grey colored fondant and texture it with a 'corrugated' textured mat or ruler. Affix the fondant to the roof panels with royal icing.

6. Next, make the colored piping/eaves for the roof. Roll the fondant between your palms to make an even sausage shape and cut it to length or use a clay extruder for a guaranteed even finish – affix these with royal icing after allowing them to dry a little to ensure they hold their shape.

7. To make the doors, roll out fondant in a matching color to your eaves and cut an appropriate sized rectangle (no more than ⅔ the side of your front panel for visual balance). Emboss vertical lines to indicate a wooden door by using a ruler or the back of a paring knife and affix with royal

icing. From the scraps of rolled fondant cut long triangles to make hinges and use sugar glue to affix them to the door. Once dry and hard paint over them with edible silver plaint (or rusty-copper metallic paint for a weathered look) to indicate the metal hinges and door handle and lock for authenticity.

8. To make the pebbles can be time consuming, but it's definitely worth it, it looks really good! They are made by using grey and white fondant partially kneaded together. Roll each piece into a small ball and squashing the small ball down on the board, lightly covered with royal icing. Put each one up against the next to give a jumbled together pebbled beach look. If you don't have time to make the pebbles, simply cover your board in a thick layer of grey and white swirled fondant and use a texture mat to imprint pebbles.

The Unit Block

I love the idea of a snow covered unit block, all warm inside – each home going about their own thing on a cold day perfect for the indoors. Add whatever little touches make your apartment block uniquely yours.

TO MAKE THIS, YOU'LL NEED:

White fondant

Black fondant

Gel food color: black, sky blue, brown and lemon yellow

Royal icing

Piping bag and round piping tip

Display board

1 x 22 gauge (or similar) florist or cake decorators wire

A paint brush, fondant modelling tool, or toothpick to make indents in the bin

Clay extruder (optional for drain pipes)

Square cutters – small and large

Rectangle cutters

Rolling pin

Sugar glue

METHOD:

1. To make the gingerbread, follow the gingerbread recipe of your choice from the gingerbread chapter (page 8).

2. If you have not pre-cut your shapes before baking, use your templates to cut the shapes out of your fresh baked gingerbread using a small paring knife. Allow the gingerbread to cool and transfer to a wire rack to come to room temperature and stiffen a little. You can leave it over night for maximum durability. Create templates for the dimensions (below) on A4 paper. Refer to page 137 for templates. Cut the paper to the following dimensions:

   - Sides (make 4): 13cm wide x 20cm tall (5.1in x 7.8in)
   - Roof (make 1): 22cm wide x 22cm tall (8.6in x 8.6in)

3. Once the gingerbread is baked, use a brick impression mat on the gingerbread pieces while they are still quite hot.

4. Either before or after baking, use square and rectangle cutters to remove the parts that will be windows for your design. For this design, the side walls have one large and one small square cut out of each level indicating a large window to let light into a living space and a small one indicating a bathroom space. The front of the block has small squares either side representing unit windows and small rectangle windows down the center to indicate light-letting windows for a communal stairwell, as is indicated by the larger square door panel in the center of the piece at the base of these rectangle windows.

5. Make sure you have affixed your blinds and curtains and fondant indicating light over the back of these window holes and given them adequate time to dry before constructing your piece. (See page 28 for more on windows.)

6. To construct the unit block, assemble all four sides at the same time to make a cube shape. Two sides will have raw edges exposed and two sides will have no edges exposed, ensure your front of your unit block covers the edges of its adjoining sides to give it a front-facing impact.

7. Allow your shape to dry before adding the roof and ensure the royal icing securing the roof is completely dry before adding any additional decorations.

8. Make the silver trashcans in the snow by rolling grey fondant into a teardrop shape, flattening each end on a clean, dry surface by tapping it gently and then indenting the sides with the non-brush end of a small paintbrush, modelling tool or toothpick.

9. Make the lid using a circle cutter and leave both pieces to dry separately before joining them together using royal icing. Once assembled paint over the bin with edible silver paint (optional – they can stay grey) and insert them into the snow to be secured to the board.

10. To create the drain pipes along the edge of the roof

and down the sides of the building use a clay extruder; in the absence of this tool you can simply roll the grey fondant between your palms to make long fat sausage shapes. Allow this to harden slightly before trying to attach to help ensure it keeps it shape.

11. Make the antennae atop the roof by bending and twisting a piece of 22 gauge florists wire into shape, trimming off the end, inserting it into the roof after it has been constructed, and secured in place with royal icing.

12. Finally, to cover the board in snow use a piping tip and a spatula – allowing the piped log look to remain closer to the path to appear like it has been shovelled and using the spatula to make the rest look like recent snowfall.

Note: if you are doing a large-scale unit block you could use a ball tool to hollow out the bin, allow it to dry and fill it full of candy before attaching the lid. Alternatively you could do the same for a small bin and fill it full of Wonka Nerds! An exciting bonus for the child who takes the dare to eat the trash bin off of the gingerbread unit block!

To decorate the house, decorate with whatever candies and chocolate you prefer. You can also pipe royal icing to create decorative designs around the walls of the house and roof.

White Star Tree

The white star tree is the perfect accompaniment for your gingerbread house as the giant Christmas tree growing the back yard or as a stand alone feature for the Christmas table! This one has been made using a light gingerbread; you can make yours with several smaller batches of different flavored gingerbread for a surprising variety.

TO MAKE THIS YOU'LL NEED:

20 pieces of gingerbread (stars)

10 different sized star cutters (you can make it with a lot less –your tree will just be smaller)

White fondant

Display board

Rolling pin

Edible gold paint

METHOD:

1. To make the gingerbread, follow the gingerbread recipe of your choice from the gingerbread chapter (page 8). Allow the gingerbread to cool and transfer to a wire rack to come to room temperature and stiffen a little. You can leave it over night for maximum durability.

2. This tree is made using 10 different sized star cutters. You can use less or more depending on the size you want your tree to be. Regardless of the size you choose, it is important to make 2 of every size, this is what gives it visual and literal balance as you work from largest to smallest.

3. Using the same cutters, roll out your white fondant and cut out stars, affix the fondant stars to their corresponding sized gingerbread stars with royal icing.

4. To assemble the tree, secure the largest star to your display board with royal icing. Place a blob of royal icing in the center of this star and place a star of the same size on top of it. Be careful to alternate the points of the star so that the points of the top star point out in between the hollows of the bottom star. Repeat this step for all of your stars in descending order of size until you reach the last one.

5. The last star to be attached should be the same size as the last star you applied to the top of the tree. Using a generous amount of royal icing applied to the middle and out to the edges of the last star on top of the tree, place your final start upright into the royal icing. You may need to hold it in place for a few seconds while the royal icing starts to dry it in place.

Variations: Want to keep it green? Simply use green fondant and some royal icing to attach red Jaffas to the branches to create a decorated and very edible green Christmas tree.

Don't like fondant? To use royal icing to ice and decorate your stars, you need to use the icing method called 'flooding'. Allow these to dry before assembling them. Construct as per the above instructions.

Use your thicker royal icing to pipe small star shaped blobs (using a star tip) on the end of each bough (star point) of the tree.

TIPS: Make sure you rollout your gingerbread dough evenly – any variation in thickness can put the entire tree off kilter.

Try and make these cookies a bit fatter than you normally would – they need to hold the weight of the cookies stacked on top of them and a thicker size will help to avoid breakages.

Keep your fondant toppers quite thin as the color contrast will have a great effect and making it too thick will make the tree look disproportionate.

Russian Dollhouse

I love the Russian Babushka (matryoshka /nesting) dolls, and the contrast between the luminous red of the doll and the dark rich gingerbread is just too good to resist! While these dolls do not nest and are nowhere near as detailed or beautiful as the originals, I could not resist a modern simple little Russian doll with matching dollhouse. The dolls can be made any size you like – super small, to scale with the house, or a lot larger to be individual cookie gifts – they are ornate and pretty enough to stand alone.

TO MAKE THIS YOU'LL NEED:

4 gingerbread pieces (plus 2 for the dolls)
Fondant in red, white, black, ivory and brown.
Onlay mold
Display board
Heart cutter (small)
Blossom cutter (small)
Circle cutter – small and medium (for doll belly, face and
    door detail)
Snowflake cutter/embosser
Jaffas
Royal icing
Lollies for the center (optional)
Rolling pin
Spatula
Small round piping tip and piping bag is recommended

METHOD:

1. To make the gingerbread, follow the gingerbread recipe of your choice from the gingerbread chapter (page 8). You only need to make 4 large pieces.

2. If you have not pre-cut your shapes before baking, use your templates to cut the shapes out of your fresh baked gingerbread using a small paring knife. Allow the gingerbread to cool and transfer to a wire rack to come to room temperature and stiffen a little. You can leave it over night for maximum durability. Create templates for the dimensions (below) on A4 paper. Refer to page 138 for templates. Cut the paper to the following dimensions:

*   Front and back panel – triangular (make 2): 20cm

wide x 19cm tall (7.8in x 7.4in)
*   Roof panels (make 2): 21cm wide x 15cm tall (8.2in x 5.9in) (more if you require additional overhang of the roof)

3. When assembling this mark along the board the same width (depth) as the roof and position the front and back panels over the end of these lines. Affix them to the board with royal icing and leave a drinking glass or fondant bucket behind them to prop them up as they dry. Once the front and back panels are dry, add on the roof panels using royal icing.

Note: If you are adding a surprise inside – add one roof panel and use the gap left waiting for the last roof panel as your access point to put the surprise candies. Be careful not to fill it too much, as this may cause breakages.

Add the onlay mold detail to the roof panels before construction (see page 30 in the how to section for details). Once the roof panels have dried in place, fill the gap between the two halves of the roof with royal icing and adorn with red Jaffas to match up with the small splashes of red in the rest of the design.

4. Create the front door by rolling out a small amount of red fondant and using a paring knife to cut a large rectangle. Emboss the rectangle with a small rectangular cutter or a paring knife to create the illusion of door detail. Affix door to the front panel of the house with royal icing. Make sure the width of your rectangle door is the same

diameter of the circle cutter used for the embellishment on the top of the door – that way it fits together perfectly.

5. To make the top of the door, cut out a circle of red fondant and a circle of white fondant and cut both in half. For the white half, use a very small heart cutter and remove three small hearts from the semicircle. Allow it to dry a little, then place the white semi circle over the red one securing it with sugar glue. After allowing both items to harden slightly, affix it above the door with royal icing.

Hint: Roll out your two circles half the thickness of your door each so that way when they are glued together and positioned above the door they are the same thickness.

6. Using the remaining white fondant cut out one small snowflake using a snowflake puncher and affix it with royal icing to the top third of the front panel as the embellishment for the house.

7. Lastly, cover the board with royal icing using a spatula to create patterns in the snow and pipe larger lines of it to hold up the Russian dolls. Place them into the blobs of royal icing.

TO MAKE THE DOLLS:

1. If you can't find a cutter, don't worry, you can easily make a template by printing out a two dimensional picture of the doll to the size you need – cut it out with scissors and cut around that shape with a paring knife to make gingerbread dolls of the same.

2. Once baked and cut out, apply a coat of chocolate to the back to add an extra element of support.

3. To decorate the dolls, simply use your template and paring knife to cut the same shape out of rolled out red fondant. Before applying the red fondant to the doll, take a medium and a small sized circle cutter (relevant to the size of your doll template) and remove a small circle from the middle of the face and a medium sized one from the belly.

4. Roll out some ivory fondant as thick as you have rolled out your red fondant and cut out a small round circle, then do the same using the white fondant and a medium cutter.

Allow all three pieces to harden slightly before applying them to the cookie.

5. Place the red shape first, followed by the ivory and white circles. This should start to look more like a doll.

6. Using a very small circle cutter at a 45° angle or a smile tool (U shaped tool), indent a smile into the bottom third of the ivory circle and allow the ivory to set before adding any more detail.

7. To make the eyes, roll out two equal-sized balls of white fondant and two equal-sized balls of blue/brown fondant, slightly smaller than the white. Stack the colored fondant on top of the white and push directly downwards to create two evenly shaped, flat eyes. Next, roll two very small balls of black fondant of equal size and add them to the center of the eyes.

Cute option: Using a tooth pick and white gel food coloring, place a dot of white in the top left or top right of each black pupil – make sure it's the same side for both eyes – to create a light reflection in the doll's eyes.

TIP: You can purchase silicon molds for cartoon style eyes and edible pre-made cute eyes from cake decorating supply stores and on line.

Compass to my heart

A sweet, simple, subtle declaration of love.

TO MAKE THIS YOU'LL NEED:

6 pieces of gingerbread

Red fondant

Gel food color (forest green)

Royal icing

Display board

Small piping tip – round

Small piping tip – star

Piping bag

Metal ruler

Spatula to apply the royal icing to the board

Rolling pin

METHOD:

1. To make the gingerbread, follow the gingerbread recipe of your choice from the gingerbread chapter (page 8). You will need to make 6 gingerbread pieces.

2. This house was made using a basic, medium-sized gingerbread house cutter set. It has minimal decoration to draw attention to the feature piece – the piped north/south/east/west compass around a heart shaped keyhole above the door.

3. If you have not pre-cut your shapes before baking, use your templates to cut the shapes out of your fresh baked gingerbread using a small paring knife. Allow the gingerbread to cool and transfer to a wire rack to come to room temperature and stiffen a little. You can leave it over night for maximum durability. Create templates for the dimensions (below) on A4 paper. Refer to page 139 for templates. Cut the paper to the following dimensions:

4. Front and back panel (make 2): 10cm wide x 13cm tall (3.9in x 5.1in)*

    *   Sides (make 2): 9cm wide x 7cm tall (3.5in x 2.7in)
    *   Roof (make 2): 13.5cm wide x 10 cm tall (5.3in x 3.9in)

5. Construct the house using royal icing, starting with front, back and sides, allowing them to dry before adding the roof pieces. don't forget to pipe along the join line of the two roof pieces to cover your raw edges and give the effect of snow caught on the roof peak.

6. Create the door using a simple arch shaped cutter and very thickly rolled out red fondant. Imprint the lines using a metal ruler so the door looks as though it is made of red wood panels. Affix to the front of the house using royal icing.

7. Create the garland around the edges of the door using green royal icing piped with a star tip or a rounded tip in a circular motion. Add piped red dots as berries or try cachous in red, silver or gold – even sprinkles will work, to give it the effect of a climbing green vine in bloom.

8. To pipe the compass you can wait until the very last step to ensure its safety which requires you to pipe on an upright piece, or if you prefer to pipe on a piece laying flat – apply the compass detail before construction.

Note: handle with care as fine pieces of dry royal icing can break off if knocked or brushed hard enough.

9. Apply the remaining white royal icing to the board using a spatula, this gives the effect of snow and ties your design together.

10. Dust icing sugar over the final design for a more romantic, whimsical look.

> **TIP:** *Dont forget to remove a love heart shape form your front panel. If you are unsure of how it will turn out – take a heart shape piece from both the front and the back and put the best one at the front!

Small and Bright

A sweet, simple, small and bright twist on the Compass to my Heart. Quick and easy to make with a finish that makes quite an impression – if you are going to make a lot of little houses as gifts this design is perfect.

TO MAKE THIS YOU'LL NEED:

Fondant: white and red

Gel colors: forest green, sky blue and black
  (for grey pebbles)

Silicon mold for holly wreath (or cutters)

Royal icing

Small piping tip – round

Piping bag

Display board

Rolling pin

Metal ruler

Paring knife

Spatula to apply the royal icing to the board

Edible gold paint (optional)

METHOD:

1. To make the gingerbread, follow the gingerbread recipe of your choice from the gingerbread chapter (page 8). You will need to make 6 pieces plus enough for a gingerbread window shutters.

2. If you have not pre-cut your shapes before baking, use your templates to cut the shapes out of your fresh baked gingerbread using a small paring knife. Allow the gingerbread to cool and transfer to a wire rack to come to room temperature and stiffen a little. You can leave it over night for maximum durability. Create templates for the dimensions (below) on A4 paper. Refer to page 140 for templates. Cut the paper to the following dimensions:

  • Front and back panel of house (make 2): 10cm wide x 13cm tall (3.9in x 5.1in)
  • Sides (make 2): 9cm wide x 7cm tall (3.5in x 2.7in)
  • Roof (make 2): 13.5cm wide x 10 cm tall (5.3in x 3.9in)

3. Construct the house using royal icing, starting with front, back and sides, allowing them to dry before adding the roof pieces. Don't forget to pipe along the join line of the two roof pieces to cover your raw edges and give the effect of snow caught on the roof peak.

4. To create the door, roll out some red fondant and use a paring knife and paper template to cut the door shape. Next, use a metal ruler to add indents over the fondant to create a 'wood panelled' look. Roll out a small ball of red fondant to create the door knob, and once attached to the door paint it with edible gold paint. Using white royal icing attach the door to the front panel, using the same royal icing pipe along the top of the door for a snow caught effect.

5. Next, create the wreath above the door. Do this using a silicon mold (see how to section page 27) or holly leaf cutters and arranging them into a wreath. Add little red berries over the top of the berries already present in the mold by rolling small pieces of red fondant between your thumb and forefinger to make a ball. Secure it with sugar glue and allow to dry, this gives you wreath additional dimension and adds interest. When the wreath is dry paint over the bow with edible gold paint or if you are making your wreath, add bow to the top and paint it gold when it has dried. Secure the wreath in place with royal icing.

Note: The wreath can be replaced with two or three holly leaves with red berries or a Christmas star or even a mini Merry Christmas sign.

6. The sides of this house have windows that are easy to make. Simply, roll out some pale blue fondant thinly and cut it into rectangles with a paring knife and attach to the house using royal icing.

7. To create the shutters, use leftover pieces of gingerbread cut into rectangles and affix them with royal icing. Once dry, use royal icing to create a basic border and horizontal lines to give the effect of white shutters.

8. Between the two shutters along the border of the window is simply green royal icing piped with a rounded tip in a circular motion to make it look like greenery in window boxes. Add piped red dots as berries or try cachous in red silver or gold – even sprinkles will work, to give it the effect of greenery in bloom.

9. To make the chimney, use the same red fondant as the front door and model it into a long thick rectangle. Using the back of a paring knife, imprint lines to give the effect of brickwork. Use a ball tool to indent the top of the chimney to make it seem hollow to the first glance. Allow this to dry a little before proceeding. Cut the base of it on a sharp angle with the sharp side of the paring knife – apply royal icing to this end and place it gently onto the roof of the house – you may need to hold it in place for a few seconds to allow the royal icing time to dry. You may also need to pipe around the base of the chimney to help secure it in place. Once secured in place as a rim of white royal icing around the top of the chimney.

10. To make the path, simply mix together a small amount of black fondant or colored gel into white fondant. Roll the fondant between your palms until they colors are striated. Pick small amounts of fondant out of the ball and roll into rough pebble shapes and push them down onto the board in front of the house. Repeat until the path has been created. Pipe or apply the royal icing to the board with a spatula to create the look of snowfall on the ground at the very end. Allow it to dry before moving it.

Easter Bunny House

TIME

DIFFICULTY

As a child, I would often sit and imagine what sort of house the Easter bunny lived in and where all of those delicious chocolate eggs came from. Why not dream up your own version and make one out of gingerbread this Easter!

TO MAKE THIS YOU'LL NEED:

12 pieces gingerbread

Royal icing

Small rectangle cutter

Silicon mold/cutter/paper template and paring knife for window and door

Brick embossing mat for pathway

Silicon mold/cutter for leaves and flowers

Easter eggs

Fondant: white, black

Gel food coloring; brown, purple, black, green, pink

Piping bag and round piping tip

Sugar glue

Rolling pin

Display board

Wafers (optional)

Edible image (optional for windows)

233 grass tip (optional – for grass)

Black edible pen (optional – for name plate)

Edible gold paint (optional – for door and window trim)

Embroidery scissors (optional – for carrot tops)

METHOD:

1. To make the gingerbread, follow the gingerbread recipe of your choice from the gingerbread chapter (page 8).

2. This design is made up of house 1 and house 2. House 1 is the side with the door on it and house 2 is the side with the windows. The roof of 2 needs to fit on to/sit flush with the roof of house 1, this is why the roof measurements of house number two may seem odd shaped.

3. If you have not pre-cut your shapes before baking, use your templates to cut the shapes out of your fresh baked gingerbread using a small paring knife. Allow the gingerbread to cool and transfer to a wire rack to come

to room temperature and stiffen a little. You can leave it over night for maximum durability. Create templates for the dimensions (below) on A4 paper. Refer to page 142 for templates. Cut the paper to the following dimensions:

House 1

- Front and back (make 2): 14cm wide x 20cm tall (5.5in x 7.9in)
- Sides (make 2): 10cm wide x 11cm tall (3.9in x 4.3in)
- Roof (make 2): 14cm wide x 11cm tall (5.5in x 4.3in)

House 2

- Front and back (make 2) 14cm wide x 20cm tall (5.5in x 7.9in)
- Sides (make 2) 20cm wide x 11cm tall (7.9in x 4.3in)
- Roof (make 2) 22cm wide x 12cm tall (8.7in x 4.7in)

4. Either prior or post baking, use a small rectangle cutter or template to remove window panels. When the gingerbread has cooked you can affix an edible image to the back side of the gingerbread (see page 28 for details). Externally added windows can be made using fondant and royal icing. (See Small and Bright on page 140 for example.)

5. Construct house 2 and then construct house 1 onto the side of house 2 at a 90 degree angle. Add the roof pieces last after all of the sides have been constructed and allowed to dry fully. Option: Add wafers to the roof to look like solar panels, this is an especially useful decoration if you need to cut away a portion of a roof panel for them to fit together.

6. Create the veggie patch. The bed is made using brown fondant – simply make a ball of fondant in your hands and then, using the work surface, press each side down until it forms a solid rectangular shape. Place your pre-

made sugar vegetables and Easter eggs into the garden – securing them with melted chocolate

7. Build a stone wall around the garden bed, attaching with sugar glue (see Beach Sheds on page 63 and make the stones larger).

8. Using a silicon mold, cutter or template and paring knife, cut out your door and windows using fondant and affix to the gingerbread house using royal icing. Once dried you can paint over the handle and fixings with edible gold paint for effect.

9. Roll out your brown fondant and emboss with brick work texture mat – secure to the board with royal icing or melted chocolate, leading towards the front door to make a path.

10. Using a 233 grass tip and green royal icing, pipe around the path an garden bed and across the board to create a short mown lawn effect. Add small, pre-made flowers to the grass to give it a real spring feel. Secure the pre-made pot plant at the front door as soon as the grass is piped in that area, be generous with your piping to help secure it.

11. To make carrots, simply roll a small amount of orange fondant into a short, fat log shape. Using your little finger roll back and forth along the last third of this log, which will elongate it to a point. On the fat end, make a cut with your paring knife and insert a small piece of green fondant to act as the green tops. Cut this green fondant with sharp, long embroidery scissors to make strands.

12. To make cabbages, make small balls of green fondant and cover them with small rose petal shaped pieces of fondant (place the petal point towards the bottom). Attach by alternating sides and bending the larger round leafs outwards until it looks like cabbage.

13. To make the pot plant see instructions on the Beach House on page 41. To make the name plate you can use a silicon mold, cutter and texture mat or template and paring knife. Create your name plate and allow it to dry a little before using and edible pen to write the name of your house. Affix above the front door with royal icing.

Log Cabin

Do you prefer savory over sweet? Or are you someone who prefers a bit of salt with their sugar? Then try this! Pretzel sticks are the best thing to look like logs – light, crispy and perfectly salted they complement a less sweet gingerbread, secured in place with a thin layer of royal icing for zesty sweet tang, and they make a perfect log cabin!

TO MAKE THIS YOU'LL NEED:

9 pieces of gingerbread

2 large bags of pretzel sticks (one should suffice but buy 2 in case of a packet of breakages and to maximize your choice of stick length (plus you get to eat the leftovers!)

Royal icing

Display board

1 x pack of Cadbury Pods or chocolates of your choice

METHOD:

1. To make the gingerbread, follow the gingerbread recipe of your choice from the gingerbread chapter (page 8).

2. If you have not pre-cut your shapes before baking, use your templates to cut the shapes out of your fresh baked gingerbread using a small paring knife. Allow the gingerbread to cool and transfer to a wire rack to come to room temperature and stiffen a little. You can leave it over night for maximum durability. Create templates for the dimensions (below) on A4 paper. Refer to page 146 for templates. Cut the paper to the following dimensions:

- Base flooring: 15cm wide x 15cm tall (5.9in x 5.9in)
- Back and front wall (make 2): 13cm wide x 16cm tall (5.1in x 6.2in)
- Sides (L-shaped – refer to templates for complete dimensions) (make 2): 14cm wide x 13cm tall (5.5in x 5.1in)
- Roof option 1 (make 2): 14cm wide x 8cm tall (5.5in x 3.1in)
- Roof option 2 (deck) (make 2): 16cm wide x 14cm tall (6.2in x 5.5in)

3. First, attach your base panel piece to your board with royal icing. Build your house back, front and sides onto of this base piece and allow to dry before attaching the roof and veranda sides.

4. Once the house has been constructed and the royal icing is dry, add your roof decoration in straight lines first, then attach your pretzel sticks from the base up, one panel at a time, starting with the front panel. Attach your sticks using a small amount of royal icing applied to the gingerbread with a small spatula, pressing the pretzel stick down into the layer of royal icing to secure it. When the house is covered add Pretzel Sticks to the veranda sides and base as well as the sides of the roof to cover the raw edges.

5. Lastly, use your left over pretzel sticks to make a door and window frames. fill in the window frames with royal icing to give the effect of ice frosted glass.

6. Cover the board with royal icing to look like snow. To make footprints, simply use your knuckles to push into the snow in an alternating step pattern.

7. For the fresh falling snow look – dust icing sugar over the house when it is complete.

8. If you have time and materials (fondant and an edible pen) you can make a small, simple welcome sign for above the door. If you want to get creative, consider making a pair of boots and some fishing poles from gum paste to adorn the veranda.

Ginger Townhouse Hill

Want to make an impressive gingerbread display but don't want the hassle of lots of 3D houses?

The Ginger Townhouse Hill is simply three craft foams covered in royal icing and stuck together, then covered in a series of house fronts (individual gingerbread cookies) which create the appearance of a three-tier village on a hill. The simplicity of basic cookies with all the impact of a highly designed and constructed village. This one is perfect for the office and big family gatherings – everyone can marvel at your work and then help themselves.

TO MAKE THIS YOU'LL NEED:

1 x 20cm round x 7.6cm tall (8in x 3in) Styrofoam

1 x 15cm round x 7.6in tall (6in x 3in) Styrofoam

1 x 10cm round x 7.6 tall (4in x 3in) Styrofoam

Red and green fondant to cover the foams (optional – you can always fill-in the exposed foam parts with royal icing and cover each ledge with unattached wrapped chocolates)

Display board

Royal icing

Gel food colors (to match your color scheme)

Fondant (optional for detail on houses)

METHOD:

1. To make the gingerbread, follow the gingerbread recipe of your choice from the gingerbread chapter (page 8).

2. For this design I have simply used two cutters from two different sized gingerbread house cutter sets – using the larger houses at the base and the smaller ones towards the top. This means that there are fewer houses to make to cover the bottom and it gives the illusion of the houses getting smaller as they go up the hill.

3. If you don't have house cutters create templates, create templates for the dimensions (below) on A4 paper. Refer to page 148 for templates. Cut the paper to the following dimensions (see complete dimension for the house on top in templates):

- House front 1 (large): 14cm wide x 19cm tall (5.5in x 7.4in)

- House front 2 (small): 10cm wide x 13cm tall (3.9in x 5in)

4. Once you have baked your gingerbread and it has cooled you can start decorating. there is no wrong way to decorate your townhouses, the limit is your imagination!

5. Once your decorated townhouses are dry use royal icing or melted chocolate to secure them to the foam.

Note: For reenforcement; as detailed in the 'How to' section of the book (see page 25) you can reinforce the back of your gingerbread pieces with chocolate, chocolate bark or even toffee. for this design the foam provides support for most of your gingerbread so you only need the reinforce the back if your gingerbread recipe is soft or if you choose quite heavy decorations, like a fondant cover or lollies. See page 18 for chocolate bark recipe ideas.

> **TIP:** Put this on a hard display board (round Masonite, not cardboard), which will help keep it stable and protect your bottom ring of townhouses fronts from damage.

Hansel House

From the odd-shaped houses found in classic fairy tale stores comes so much inspiration for gingerbread houses! This one is delicately piped with a simple swirly design with all the whimsy of a fairy tale.

TO MAKE THIS YOU'LL NEED:

8 pieces of baked gingerbread

Royal icing

Gel food color – green, orange and red

Display board

Piping bag

Piping tip – rounded

Arch cutter (optional)

METHOD:

1. To make the gingerbread, follow the gingerbread recipe of your choice from the gingerbread chapter (page 8).

2. If you have not pre-cut your shapes before baking, use your templates to cut the shapes out of your fresh baked gingerbread using a small paring knife. Allow the gingerbread to cool and transfer to a wire rack to come to room temperature and stiffen a little. You can leave it over night for maximum durability. Create templates for the dimensions (below) on A4 paper. Refer to page 150 for templates. Cut the paper to the following dimensions:

- Front and back (make 2): 16cm wide x 25cm tall (6.3in x 9.8in) – this curves in to 12cm (4.7in) at thinnest point, refer to templates for directions
- Sides (make 2): 10cm wide x 14.5cm tall (3.9in x 5.7in)
- Roof (make 2): 10cm wide x 14.5cm tall (3.9in x 5.7in)

3. Construct your pieces using white royal icing, start with the back and side pieces first, allowing them to dry hard before attaching the front. Allow the royal icing to dry completely before adding the roof panels.

4. Create the door and bay window by using leftover pieces of gingerbread and a small arch cutter. If you do not have arch cutters print an arch shape onto paper and use it as a template or hand draw one.

5. The fine piping decoration on this house can be very fragile and while piping the detail after the house is constructed is the safest option, piping prior to construction provides an easier angle for greater detail and control.

6. Start by piping green, swirly lines on the front of the house, roof, door and bay window, allowing it to crust slightly before piping little, red, berry-like dots at various points across the vines to look like berries.

7. Lastly, pipe white royal icing in the crevice of the roof, along the sides of the roof and across the tops of the door and window to look like snow and cover your raw-edges. Using the remainder of the royal icing and a spatula, cover your display board to complete your look.

TIP: When dying royal icing red, it is best to dye it orange first, this neutralizes the white color, providing a base color to reflect the red and eliminates the need to move through the pink spectrum to achieve a nice deep Christmas red color – you also use less dye!

The Family Home

Sweet and traditional – who doesn't love a gingerbread family and their family home! Adorned with as many chocolates and lollies as you can find, this is a gingerbread dream house! This has been made with one man and one woman to demonstrate one of each – mix this up to represent your own family – this is definitely a project that the kids will love to participate in!

TO MAKE THIS YOU'LL NEED:

Fondant or royal icing (to decorate as many gingerbread people as you like)
Rolling pin
Display board
Sprinkles for the board
Wafers
Chocolate bullets
Freckles for the roof
100's and 1000's
Licorice logs

METHOD:

1. To make the gingerbread, follow the gingerbread recipe of your choice from the gingerbread chapter (page 8).
2. If you have not pre-cut your shapes before baking, use your templates to cut the shapes out of your fresh baked gingerbread using a small paring knife. Allow the gingerbread to cool and transfer to a wire rack to come to room temperature and stiffen a little. You can leave it over night for maximum durability. Create templates for the dimensions (below) on A4 paper. Refer to page 152 for templates. Cut the paper to the following dimensions:
   - Front and back panel (make 2): 13cm wide x 19cm tall (5in x 7.4in)
   - Sides (make 2): 21cm wide x 13cm tall (8.2in x 5in)
   - Roof (make 2): 25cm wide x 11 cm tall (9.8in x 4.3in)
   - Doorway front: 8cm wide x 13cm tall (3in x 5in)

Gingerbread Family
   - To create your gingerbread family, you can either use a set of cutters (can be purchased at craft and baking

stores), or create paper templates yourself to suit your family.

Note: Always make double! That way, if there is a breakage you have an immediate replacement, and if not, you have some sneaky snacks for yourself!

3. Construct the house sides and front and allow the royal icing to dry before adding the roof.
4. The family can be decorated using rolled out colored fondant or piping – you can use a combination of both of these mediums or chose one only – see the how to section (page 29) for all your piping options.
5. To decorate the house, decorate with whatever lollies and chocolate you prefer. for this design I have used freckles for the roof, chocolate bullets and 100's and 1000's for the door and wafers for the walls. I have secured these to each panel after construction and have used melted chocolate to secure them.
6. Cover the board with melted chocolate and add your licorice log pathway first, then add sprinkles immediately so they are secured to the board as the chocolate sets.
7. I have used Royal icing to secure the gingerbread family to board last, as royal icing will set them in place more securely than chocolate. If your gingerbread family is heavy with decoration you can pop a ball of fondant behind them to prop them up and cover it over with royal icing.

3D Reindeer

Want to make your Christmas cookies a bit different this year? try going 3D! Gift them in a clear plastic box with a simple ribbon – Christmas gift sorted!

TO MAKE THIS YOU'LL NEED:

Circle pastry cutters (size 98mm) scalloped edge

Display board

Christmas tree cutter or paper template

Reindeer cutter or paper template

Fondant; white, green and brown

Edible image (optional)

Royal icing

Rounded piping tip

Piping bag

Sugar glue

Rolling pin

Silver cashous

Cake lace

Ball tool

METHOD:

1. To make the gingerbread, follow the gingerbread recipe of your choice from the gingerbread chapter (page 8).

2. Using the scalloped side of the double-sided pastry cutter (98mm), cut out 1 large gingerbread cookie. Then, use a reindeer cutter and Christmas tree cutter to cut a gingerbread cookie.

Note: Make sure they are in proportion to the size of the scalloped edge cookie you are sticking them to.

3. Decorate all 3 pieces individually before assembling them. Roll and cut white fondant with the same scalloped edge cutter that you used for the cookie, apply the fondant to the cookie using royal icing. Coat the fondant in a small thin layer of sugar glue to help secure the cake lace (see page 30 for cake lace details).

4. Use the same process for the green tree, cutting away the green base to leave space for your brown fondant to be attached to give the impression of a tree trunk. If you want to add cashous to look like baubles, use your ball tool to make indents into the fondant while it is soft, then using a small round piing tip, pipe a small amount of royal icing into these depressions before adding cashous. Allow this to dry before standing up right. For the reindeer I have purchased an image printed onto edible paper. Cut around the image to make the same shape as the cookie. Cover the cookie with white fondant first to for a base and then affix the image to the fondant with sugar glue.

5. Once your gingerbread cookies are decorated attach the tree upright on the back third of the larger cookie, which is laying flat. Secure the reindeer next to and slightly in front of the tree so it is prominent.

6. You can secure the base cookie to a display board covered with royal icing, or if these are individual gifts, you can use a blob of royal icing in the Centre of the underside of the cookie to secure it to a much smaller board and cello wrap or box it to make a lovely gift.

TIP: If you are making a few of these and want to incorporate multiple flavors you can make the base, tree and reindeer from three different recipes.

Fairy Garden

A fun one to make with the kids. This design can be Christmas – themed or left as it is. It is also the perfect gingerbread house to fill with a surprise!

TO MAKE THIS YOU'LL NEED:

6 pieces of baked gingerbread

Display board

Rolling pin

Royal icing

Fondant; red and white

Gel food color in: green, pink, yellow, red and orange

Piping tip – round

Piping tip – star

Piping bag

Edible ink pen

Flower cutters

Leaf cutters

Butterfly cutters

small arch cutter or template

Edible gold paint (optional)

Silicon mold, cutter or template and paring knife for door
  and windows

Edible glitter (optional)

METHOD:

1. To make the gingerbread, follow the gingerbread recipe of your choice from the gingerbread chapter (page 8).

2. If you have not pre-cut your shapes before baking, use your templates to cut the shapes out of your fresh baked gingerbread using a small paring knife. Allow the gingerbread to cool and transfer to a wire rack to come to room temperature and stiffen a little. You can leave it over night for maximum durability. Create templates for the dimensions (below) on A4 paper. Refer to page 154 for templates. Cut the paper to the following dimensions:

- Front and back panel (make 2): 10cm wide x 15cm tall (3.9in x 5.9in) – reaches 12cm (12.7in) at thickest point, see template for details

- Side panels (make 2): 8.5cm wide x 9cm tall (3.3in x 3.5in)

- Roof panels (make 2): 12.5cm wide and 7.5–9cm tall (more if you require additional overhang of the roof) (4.9in x 2.9–3.5in)

3. Construct the side panels first allowing the royal icing to harden before adding the roof. For this design you do not need to reinforce the walls as the shape lends itself to support, however if you intend to decorate it heavily with fondant or significant flowers on the outside it is best to reinforce the walls with a thin coat of chocolate or toffee.

4. To decorate, first add the archway door, windows and shingle to the front and side panels. These have been made using brown fondant in a silicon mold and dusted with edible luster powder. You can make the hinges and handles gold by painting by edible gold paint.

5. Use and edible ink pen to draw a love heart shape from either side of the archway door. This gives you a guide to place your cut leaves and flowers, affixing them with royal icing, making them look like they have grown into a heart-shaped vine. Alternatively you can pipe these with royal icing.

6. Cover the raw edges of your roof and sides with the same vine. Cut a few extra leaves and set aside to use with your flowers.

7. To make the flowers and leaves, use various cutters and cutter/embossers in a variety of colors and attach them flat to the roof with royal icing. To make the flowers 3D, turn your fondant into gum paste (see page 27) and allow the flower to dry in a flower forming cup, egg carton or propped up in a dish made of aluminium foil. Make a flat 2D one to affix to the roof and affix the dried 3D gum paste one over the top of it with royal icing – the flat one will give a shadow effect. Make, dry and apply your butterflies in the same way. Use the additional leaves you have made

to complement the flowers and break up the bright colors.

8. Using a star tip and white royal icing – pipe into the center of the flowers to give the effect of stamen and pollen. You may wish to sprinkle edible glitter onto the wet royal icing for a shimmery effect.

9. Lastly, cover the display board with your white royal icing. Add white or colored sequins or sprinkles to the royal icing while it is still well for extra texture. Once it is dry you can sprinkle edible glitter across the board for an extra shine and magical touch!

Other roof options:

1. Pipe the flowers and leaves onto the roof using a flooding technique.

2. If you can paint, Cover your roof panels with white fondant and allow it to set. Using edible gel or paste food color mixed with water or Cake Decorator's Rose Spirit freehand paint your floral design. The water mix will give you a watercolor effect and the rose spirit mix will give you a more clear, bright and defined look.

Chinese Garden

I love Chinese botanical gardens; they are so pretty and neat. This one is taking inspiration from these beautiful, well-cared for gems but is a bit messier to make!

TO MAKE THIS YOU'LL NEED:

12 pieces of gingerbread

Display board

Red gum paste

Edible gold paint

Brown fondant or white fondant with brown gel food coloring

Blue oil based food coloring (chocolate food coloring)

233 grass tip

Piping bag

Dark chocolate

White chocolate

Small flower cutters

Metal ruler

Small spatula

Black gel food color (to make grey fondant pebbles)

Green gel food color

Royal icing

22 gauge florists wire

Paring knife

Rolling pin

Large circle cutters

Small circle cutters

METHOD:

1. To make the gingerbread, follow the gingerbread recipe of your choice from the gingerbread chapter (page 8).

2. If you have not pre-cut your shapes before baking, use your templates to cut the shapes out of your fresh baked gingerbread using a small paring knife. Allow the gingerbread to cool and transfer to a wire rack to come to room temperature and stiffen a little. You can leave it over night for maximum durability. Create templates for the dimensions (below) on A4 paper. Refer to page 156 for templates. Cut the paper to the following dimensions:

The Entrance Way

- Large circle cutter: 98mm (3.8in)
- Smaller circle cutter: 68mm (2.7in)
- Length of line across the bottom: 20cm (7.9in)
- Length of line across the top: 20cm (7.9in)

Note: It is highly advisable to reinforce this shape (with chocolate or toffee) as it will be standing alone, supported only by royal icing at the bottom.

The House Base

- Largest Rectangle: 20cm wide x 17cm tall (7.9in x 6.7in)
- Medium Rectangle: 15cm wide x 12cm tall (5.9in x 4.7in)
- Smallest Rectangle: 13cm wide x 10cm tall (5.1in x 3.9in)

The House
Level 1

- Front and Back Panel (make 2): 15cm wide x 7cm tall (5.9in x 2.8in)
- Sides (make 2): 10cm wide x 7cm tall (3.9in x 2.8in)
- Roof: 15cm wide x 12cm tall (5.9in x 4.7in)

Level 2

- Front and Back Panel (make 2): 13cm wide x 7cm tall (5.1in x 2.8in)
- Sides (make 2): 8cm wide x 7cm tall (3.1in x 2.8in)
- Roof (make 1): 13cm wide x 10cm tall (5.1in x 3.9in)

3. Start construction by securing your base piece to the back center of the display board with melted chocolate or

royal icing. Roll out your brown fondant fairly thick and emboss it with your wood grain texture mat. Cut it to the same size as your base piece and secure it with royal icing. Once the base piece is dry and secure, construct the front, back and sides of the first level. Allow this to dry before attaching the roof. As soon as the roof is attached you may secure the red roof (see point 5 below) and allow both to dry.

4. Once both are dry construct the font back and sides of level 2, allowing them enough time to dry you can add the roof piece and decoration together. Allow these to dry before adding further detail to the house.

5. To make the red roof decoration, add tylose to red fondant or using red gum paste – roll it out and cut it the same width as the roof piece and 4cm (1.6in) longer. Affix to the roof by applying a thin coat of royal icing over the gingerbread and position it so 2cm (0.8in) of gum paste hangs over either end. Smooth in place and quickly roll up the ends, secure them in place around a pen or other long, light round object placed at the edge of the gingerbread roof. Allow to dry stiff before removing.

6. Repeat step 5 for the roof of the 2nd level. With your left over red gum paste, mold an angled trapezium with your hands using a flat non stick surface, when you are happy with the shape, use a metal ruler to emboss lines across the front and back panels for texture effect.

7. Create the red lanterns using red gum paste rolled into a ball and textured by rolling over a rough surface. Use your small circle cutter to emboss a circle at the top and bottom of your lantern, paint inside these circles with edible gold paint. Using a sharp paring knife, cut off ⅕ of the back of the lantern – this creates a flat surface to make contact with the gingerbread front panel. Secure in place using royal icing.

8. To make the door you can use a silicon mold, cutter or roll out brown fondant, using your wood grain texture mat to emboss a pattern. Cut out the door to the required size, using the back of your paring knife to emboss a line down the center to represent two doors closed. Secure your door to the front of the first level. Roll a thin flat piece of brown fondant and cut it into a rectangular strip. Secure this strip to the top of the doors with sugar glue. Lastly to make the handles; make two small pea sized balls of fondant. Squash them flat with your fingers and using a ball tool make depressions in the center. Attach with sugar glue and paint in edible gold.

Note: Do not use too much royal icing to attach the door or it may sag under its own weight.

9. To make the window slats on level two, roll out your brown fondant thinly. Using a small rectangle cutter, remove three sections. Allow the fondant to stiffen a little before affixing to the gingerbread with royal icing.

10. Lastly, add your gate to the board using royal icing as it will set quicker than melted chocolate. You will need to support the back of your gate piece to remain upright while the royal icing sets.

11. Pre-prepare your grey pebbles by mixing black fondant or black gel food color into white fondant. (See Beach Sheds on page 136 for details.)

12. Next, apply the blue chocolate 'water' to the board to create a moat. To make the water I have melted down white compound chocolate and added blue oil based food coloring. Once mixed through use a spatula to apply the chocolate to the board in the area/pattern you wish your water to flow. Once applied secure the grey pebbles to the edge of the water immediately so they are stuck to the board as the chocolate sets.

13. The trees were made using 22 gauge florist's wire bent and twisted into the shape of a topiary tree and dipped into chocolate to give it a bark like texture, leaving a 3cm (1in) undipped tail. This raw wire is bent into a hook and secured to the board by inserting the base of the tree into a ball of fondant.

14. To make the trees, bend and fold 22 gauge food safe wires until they look like branches. Dip your shape into melted dark chocolate and give it a bark like texture. Secure to the board by inserting the base of the tree into a ball of fondant.

15. Using green royal icing and a 233 grass tip – pipe grass across the remaining part of the board including up and over the 'hill' created by the ball of fondant holding up the tree.

16. Cut our a small strip of brown fondant and a dozen or more little pink cherry blossoms. Secure small blossoms to the tree using royal icing. Affix the brown banner to the front of the gate and secure one blossom to the center using royal icing.

TIPS: Don't want to fuss with the board? Place some blue fondant down for water and cover the rest in royal icing snow! Leave the trees white and pipe some small blossoms on the ends et voilà – a winter garden!

If your lantern is too heavy you can help secure the two using food safe wire, just be sure to have all pieces removed and accounted for prior to eating.

The Cake Shop

There is something so magical and charming about sweet shops in old Victorian buildings. This is one of the more complicated designs, but it is really versatile.

TO MAKE THIS YOU'LL NEED:

19 pieces of gingerbread plus steps

Display board

Plaque cutter or template

Royal icing

Round piping tip

Piping bag

Edible pen or edible image (for the shop signage)

Fondant; white, red

Colored fondant or gel food coloring; blue, brown, green, pink

Sugar glue

Paring knife

Brick work texture mat

Small rectangle cutter

Small circle or arch cutter

Circle cutters in 3 sizes (for mini cakes)

Small heart cutter

Rolling pin

METHOD:

1. To make the gingerbread, follow the gingerbread recipe of your choice from the gingerbread chapter (page 8).

2. If you have not pre-cut your shapes before baking, use your templates to cut the shapes out of your fresh baked gingerbread using a small paring knife. Allow the gingerbread to cool and transfer to a wire rack to come to room temperature and stiffen a little. You can leave it over night for maximum durability. Create templates for the dimensions (below) on A4 paper. Refer to page 160 for templates. Cut the paper to the following dimensions:

Bakery

- Front and back (make 2): 15cm wide x 25cm tall (5.9in x 9.8in)
- Sides (make 2): 18cm wide x 20cm tall (7in x 7.8in) – remember one of these sides is going to be the wall behind the shop front.
- Roof (make 2): 20cm wide x 11cm tall (7.8in x 4.3in)
- Assemble these pieces of the bakery starting the front back and sides first and then roof, allowing it to dry between additions and before attaching the shop front.

Shop Front

- Front panels with large window cut outs (make 2): 7cm wide x 18cm tall (2.7in x 7in)
- Side panels (make 4): 6cm wide x 18cm tall
- (2.3in x 7in)
- Flat roof over shop front: 7cm wide x 21cm tall
- (2.7in x 8.2in)

Ornate Triangles and Peaked Roof

- Dual Triangle Piece (make 2): 20cm wide x 7cm tall (7.8in x 2.7in)
- Short Roof panels (make 2): 7cm wide x 6cm tall (2.7in x 2.3in)
- Long roof panels (make 2): 9.5cm wide x 6cm tall (3.7in x 2.3in)

3. Assemble these pieces of the bakery starting the front back and sides first and then roof, allowing it to dry between additions and before attaching the shop front.

4. Construct the shop windows one at a time. Each starting from the very edge of the wall, add the sides and then fit the front over the side panels. Once you have made 2 of these you should have a gap in the middle 5–6cm (1.9–2.3in) wide in which you can decorate as a doorway.

Allow these to dry before affixing the flat roof over both of the shop windows and front doorway. Allow the royal icing on the flat roof to set before proceeding with the ornate triangles and peaked roof.

5. To assemble, attach the two-triangle piece in place first and then attach the roof panels. Don't worry too much if the roof panels meet imperfectly you can cover this when decorating.

6. To decorate, start with the multi-layer cake. Roll out the brown colored fondant thickly and cut out 3-4 small circles using three different sized cutters. Set aside to dry.

7. Next, roll out your white fondant half the thickness of the brown. Cut out enough circles of all three sizes to fit between the brown layers. Using sugar glue to secure the circles stack the brown and white circles on top of each other, starting with brown 'cake' and alternating each layer with white 'cream', stack the tiers largest to smallest on top securing with sugar glue.

8. Lastly, roll out a small thin strip of red fondant and roll it up on a slight angle. Trim the base and secure it to the cake with sugar glue to look like rose decorations. Using the same circle cutters, roll out your white fondant very thick and cut out one of each size. Stick the three tiers together with sugar glue and make and attach pale pink roses as described for the chocolate layer cake. Make two boxed platforms from left over fondant. Make this the same height as the at the bottom of the window. You may wish to paint it silver with edible paint. Secure the cake to the top with sugar glue and allow to dry.

9. To make the sign, use a plaque cutter or paper template and cut out your fondant. Allow it to dry and use an edible ink pen to write a message. Alternatively you could use an edible image as I have here.

10. The steps to the front door have been made using small off cuts of gingerbread cut into rectangles. First, line up 3 logs horizontally, securing them to the board with royal icing. Then attach 2 more atop of the three and then 1 more atop the second steps. Attach the second and third step to the house itself with royal icing as well. Before placing the third and last step, I attach my front door so that I can ensure there will be no gap.

11. Next, make the front door using fondant. Simply roll out the fondant fairly thickly, then using a rectangle cutter or paring knife emboss the little rectangles into the door for detail. (You can repeat this on a larger scale on the side of the house to make a kitchen door.)

12. To make the white detail, roll out your white fondant and cut it to the same size as the blue door. Using a circle cutter, cut away ¾ of the door by using the top portion of the circle cutter twice on an angle so the cut out looks heart shaped.

13. Next, use a small heart shaped cutter to remove two hearts from the top corners of the white detail. Secure the white to the blue with sugar glue and the whole door to the gingerbread using a thin layer of royal icing. Then make a small ball of white fondant and attach as a door knob with royal icing.

14. Finally, use some brown fondant, roll out and emboss it with your brickwork texture mat. Cut it into a long rectangle and secure to the board with royal icing. Then use your remaining white royal icing to cover your display board. Dust your final design with icing sugar for a fresh falling snow effect.

Lolly House

Not just a pretty face – this lolly and chocolate encrusted gingerbread house will have everyone wanting to break into it and eat it! Using some basic piping techniques around the candies and chocolates we bring a touch of the old style gingerbread designs under a roof of everyone's favorite sweet treats.

TO MAKE THIS YOU'LL NEED:

6 pieces of gingerbread

Display board

Royal icing

Round piping tip (2 different types for effect)

Piping bag

Gel food color; orange, red and leaf green
  (optional if you want colored piped lines)

Lollies and chocolates of your choice

Sprinkles (optional)

METHOD:

1. To make the gingerbread, follow the gingerbread recipe of your choice from the gingerbread chapter (page 8).

2. If you have not pre-cut your shapes before baking, use your templates to cut the shapes out of your fresh baked gingerbread using a small paring knife. Allow the gingerbread to cool and transfer to a wire rack to come to room temperature and stiffen a little. You can leave it over night for maximum durability. Create templates for the dimensions (below) on A4 paper. Refer to page 164 for templates. Cut the paper to the following dimensions:

  • Front and back (make 2): 15cm wide x 19cm tall
    (5.9in x 7.5in)
  • Sides (make 2): 11cm wide x 10cm tall (4.3in x 3.9in)
  • Roof (make 2): 12cm wide x 14cm tall (4.7in x 5.5in)

3. It is best to decorate each panel prior to construction, allowing for adequate drying time before assembly.

4. Prepare your red and green royal icing piping bags. Have an idea of the design you want to pipe close to hand for visual reference. Start by securing your lollies/chocolates to each panel and then, one panel at a time,

pipe your swirly designs from the lolly outwards.

5. When your designs are dry, use white royal icing to construct the front, back and sides. Once these are dry add your roof pieces. note these will likely be heavy and may need support until they are dried in place.

6. Lastly, use your left over white royal icing to cover the display board in white snow – you may add matching colored sprinkles to the wet board so they dry in place, to carry the theme all the way through your design.

> **TIPS:** If you want an intricate, detailed pattern such as paisley or a mandala, you can draw it onto the bread using an edible pen before piping to ensure you get the detail and proportions correct.

Simple Lolly House

The sweetest of the sweet! A small little house made of lollies and gingerbread, easy to make with kids, or to delight the child within us all! This little gem is as fun to make as it is to eat.

TO MAKE THIS YOU'LL NEED:

6 pieces of gingerbread

Display board

Ginger jam cookies or fondant; white and red

Small heart cutter

Square wafers

Chocolate covered licorice

Smarties

Sprinkles

Royal icing

Candy canes

Redskins

Piping bag and round piping tip

METHOD:

1. To make the gingerbread, follow the gingerbread recipe of your choice from the gingerbread chapter (page 8).

2. If you have not pre-cut your shapes before baking, use your templates to cut the shapes out of your fresh baked gingerbread using a small paring knife. Allow the gingerbread to cool and transfer to a wire rack to come to room temperature and stiffen a little. You can leave it over night for maximum durability. Create templates for the dimensions (below) on A4 paper. Refer to page 166 for templates. Cut the paper to the following dimensions:

- Front and back panel of house (make 2): 13cm wide x 19cm tall (5.1in x 7.4in)
- Sides (make 2): 15cm wide x 13cm tall (5.9in x 5.1in)
- Roof (make 2): 17cm wide x 11cm tall (6.7in x 4.3in)

3. Construct the front, back and sides of the house, securing each piece with royal icing and allow them to dry completely before attaching the roof. Allow the roof to dry in place before adding heavy decorations.

4. Using royal icing to fill in the joining peak of the roof, lay two candy canes end to end (trim if required) with the hook end facing upwards.

5. You can achieve the roof look one of 2 ways; cut out red and white circles of fondant (same size), removing small heart shapes from the center of each white circle with a small cutter. Secure the white circles over the top of the red with sugar glue and attach them to roof using a thin layer of royal icing. Alternatively you can make small round gingerbread cookies with a heart cut from the center, once baked you can attach them to the roof with royal icing and pipe jam into the empty heart shape holes.

6. Pipe along the raw edge of the roof and sides of the house with royal icing, attaching Jaffas as you go.

7. Give the impression of windows by attaching square wafers to the gingerbread with royal icing. The windows on the side of the house have been bordered by smarties set into piped royal icing. The windows on the front of the house have had royal icing pied along the sides and dipped into a small container of sprinkles before being secured to the front of the house – this gives the illusion of busy window frames.

8. Below the windows on the side of the house the impression of a window box in bloom has been created by piping royal icing on one side of a redskin, dipping it into sprinkles and attaching it beneath the wafter windows with royal icing.

9. The front door has been made using chocolate covered licorice and smarties into a rectangle of royal icing.

10. The pathway has been made by using freckles, caramel drops and chocolate buds pushing into a layer of royal icing leading from the front doorway.

11. The rest of the display board has been covered in plain white royal icing to look like snow and provide blank space to draw attention to the busy nature of the design. use your favorite lollies and chocolates and enjoy the eating!

Mug Houses

Sweet, little bite-sized gingerbread houses that fit snug to the side of your mug! Perfect to have on hand for a spicy-sweet treat with your coffee on a cold day or as little gifts! These sweet little numbers are so easy to make and fun to decorate! Get in the spirit of the season and make a batch yourself!

TO MAKE THIS YOU'LL NEED:

6 mini pieces of gingerbread

Cup or mug (preferably with a thin rim)

Royal icing

Fine round piping tip (#1 or #2)

Sprinkles or decorations of your choice (optional)

METHOD:

1. To make the gingerbread, follow the gingerbread recipe of your choice from the gingerbread chapter (page 8).

2. If you have not pre-cut your shapes before baking, use your templates to cut the shapes out of your fresh baked gingerbread using a small paring knife. Allow the gingerbread to cool and transfer to a wire rack to come to room temperature and stiffen a little. You can leave it over night for maximum durability. Create templates for the dimensions (below) on A4 paper. Refer to page 168 for templates. Cut the paper to the following dimensions::

- Front and back (make 2): 3cm wide x 4cm tall (1.2in x 1.6in)
- Sides (make 2): 2cm wide x 2.5cm tall (0.8in x 1in)
- Roof (make 2): 2.5cm wide x 2.5cm tall (1in x 1in)

3. Construct your mini house using royal icing, allowing the front back and sides to dry before attaching the roof.

4. Once your houses are together, and dry, you can decorate them! There are so many ways to decorate these but a few basic techniques are as follows:

5. Construct your house and leave it plain – let the ginger flavors speak for themselves!

6. Using a fine piping tip (#1 rounded) and royal icing – pipe a patterned design on your house.

7. Coat the roof in white royal icing to look like it is covered in snow.

8. Dip the roof in chocolate – take the liberty to flavor and color the chocolate.

9. Dip the roof in toffee – leave it clear or color it up with your gel colors .

10. Use cake sprinkles, edible pearls, crushed candy canes, crushed nuts, edible glitter and attach them to the roof of the house by first coating the roof in either melted chocolate, royal icing or toffee and dipping the roof into a small container of your chosen sprinkles!

Note: be sure to remove a rectangle the size the rim of your mug from the center of both the front and back panels so your mini house can snugly hug your mug! To make sure it is the right size, make one test piece first and try it out on a mug/cup roughly the size you intend to use.

TIPS: These houses are sweet but are very little and piped details are especially fragile. If you are gifting these or travelling with them, secure them to a mini display board, all be it temporarily and wrap the board in cellophane tying it at the top to protect it, or alternatively place it in a tissue lined small gift box.

TeePee Mini and Maxi

TIME

DIFFICULTY

With the rise in popularity of play areas and quiet reading zones for kids, the humble TeePee is making a comeback and quite frankly they are just so damn cute! Make them as an addition to your sweets table for gender neutral baby showers or as take home party favors – the gingerbread TeePee is not just for Christmas

TO MAKE THIS YOU'LL NEED:

8 pieces of gingerbread

Display board

Royal icing

Round piping tip

Piping bag

Pretzel sticks (optional)

Cake lace (optional)

METHOD:

1. To make the gingerbread, follow the gingerbread recipe of your choice from the gingerbread chapter (page 8).

2. If you have not pre-cut your shapes before baking, use your templates to cut the shapes out of your fresh baked gingerbread using a small paring knife. Allow the gingerbread to cool and transfer to a wire rack to come to room temperature and stiffen a little. You can leave it over night for maximum durability. Create templates for the dimensions (below) on A4 paper. Refer to page 169 for templates. Cut the paper to the following dimensions:

MINI

- You will need 8 of the following triangles: 4cm wide x 10cm tall (1.6in x 3.9in)

MAXI

- You will need 8 of the following triangles: 8cm wide x 20cm tall (3.1in x 7.8in)

3. Once the shapes are cut, cut an archway out of one panel to make a door, or you may like to cut a corner flap from one of the triangles and glue it to the same panel to indicate an open flap.

4. Assembling so many triangles is quite fiddly. To make it easier assemble the shape by leaning two panels opposite each other, add the next two panels 90 degrees to the first two panels and then fill in the gaps. Have each edge of each triangle piped with white royal icing before you commence placement so that when you have them in place they begin drying.

MINI:

5. The mini teepee has been decorated using only white royal icing and a fine piping tip to make some basic patterns. This show cases the gingerbread panels as the focal point of the design.

MAXI:

6. This teepee has had every second panel covered first in cake lace feathers and doily designs. These have been secured with a thin layer of royal icing. (See page 30 for cake lace instructions.)

7. Lastly, cut three small pieces of pretzel sticks and place them into a fresh blob of white royal icing on top of the teepee. Use your remaining white royal icing to cover your display board.

TIPS: If your teepee is being transported or filled with a surprise swag of lollies or soft filling, it is advisable to coat the inside of the teepee after construction with either toffee, royal icing or melted chocolate to provide added reinforcement against breakages.

The Barn

The most simple, easy gingerbread house is an open-fronted stable, Make your fence out of chocolate or lollies for a quick simple design or challenge yourself with a gingerbread fence. This design lends itself to a Christmas themed manger, farm animals or even a horse stable in springtime.

TO MAKE THIS YOU'LL NEED:

4 pieces of gingerbread plus fence/gates

Set of plastic horses/plastic animals/manger figurines

Display board

Desiccated coconut

Gel food color; lemon yellow and leaf green

Royal icing

Piping bag

Rounded tip

Fence cutter or template & paring knife

233 grass tip (optional)

METHOD:

1. To make the gingerbread, follow the gingerbread recipe of your choice from the gingerbread chapter (page 8).

2. If you have not pre-cut your shapes before baking, use your templates to cut the shapes out of your fresh baked gingerbread using a small paring knife. Allow the gingerbread to cool and transfer to a wire rack to come to room temperature and stiffen a little. You can leave it over night for maximum durability. Create templates for the dimensions (below) on A4 paper. Refer to page 170 for templates. Cut the paper to the following dimensions:

- The back piece (make 1): 20cm wide x 8cm tall (7.8in x 3.1in)
- The sides (make 2): 10cm wide x 12cm tall one edge 8cm tall other edge (3.9in x 4.7in/3.1in)
- The roof (make 1): 14cm wide x 14cm tall (5.5in x 5.5in)

3. Construct the back and sides of the barn first and allow the royal icing to dry before adding the roof. Because the structure its taller at the front than it is at the back you may need to place a temporary support at the back of the structure to hold the roof in place while the royal icing dries.

4. The front is decorated with fences. To make these, use a fence cutter or, in the absence of a fence cutter, make one long rectangular piece and using a small rectangle and square cutter, removing dough so that it will resemble the fence palings.

Note: If you do this, consider making several smaller rectangles and fitting them together as one large piece with so much dough removed will be very fragile.

5. As the inhabitants of the stable are made of plastic/wood, and the stable is meant to be quite basic, so this design doesn't require much decoration after construction.

6. To get the golden yellow straw in the stable, mix golden yellow food color through a cup of desiccated coconut and royal icing separately, once you have done this, mix half of the golden yellow royal icing through the coconut, then quickly apply the rest to the display board inside the barn only. Using a clean spatula apply a small amount of white royal icing to the front of the barn and using your hands spread the yellow coconut-royal icing mixture out all over the barn floor and coming out of the barn slightly.

7. If you are adding plastic figurines to the inside of your barn, do so after you have added the straw. Work quickly before your Royal icing sets. Using a spatula apply royal icing to the rest of the display board in sections, adding edible and plastic items such as fences, gates and other figurines as you go.

8. If you want to add hints of grass peaking through the snow, use a 233 grass tip and green royal icing –

alternatively you can make this a spring/summer piece and pipe grass instead of snow across the board (see page 41 The Beach House).

9. Finally, pipe your snow detail across the roof and top of the fence with your white royal icing.

TIP: If you would like the effect of a gate you can either prop one panel of your fence open to indicate a gate or simply had a lock and hinges to one panel of the gate following the instructions in Beach Huts (see page 63).

HOUSE
TEMPLATES

The Button House

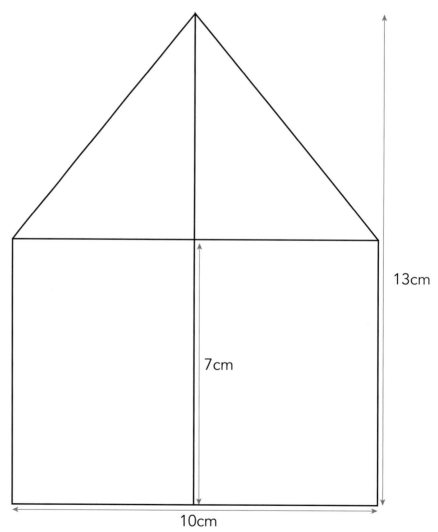

13cm

7cm

10cm

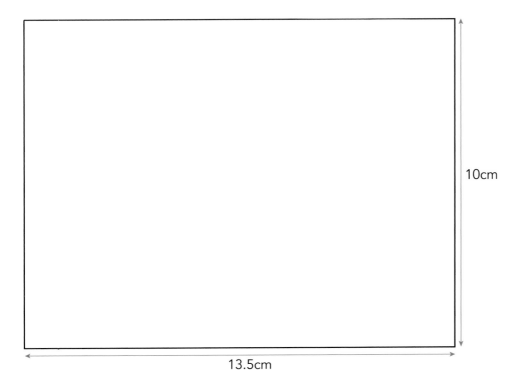

10cm

13.5cm

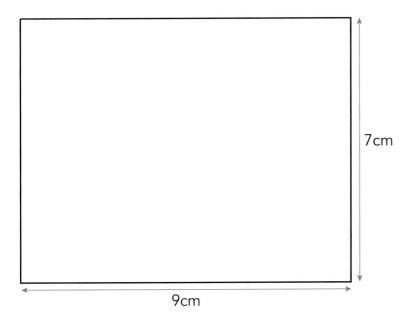

7cm

9cm

The Church

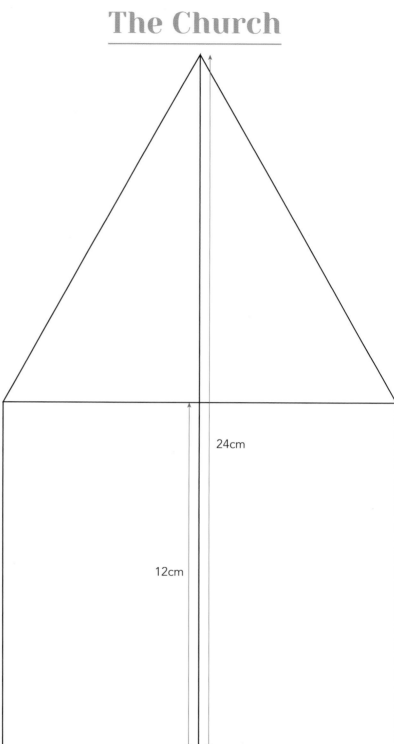

24cm

12cm

14cm

12cm

17cm

14cm

19cm

The Beach House

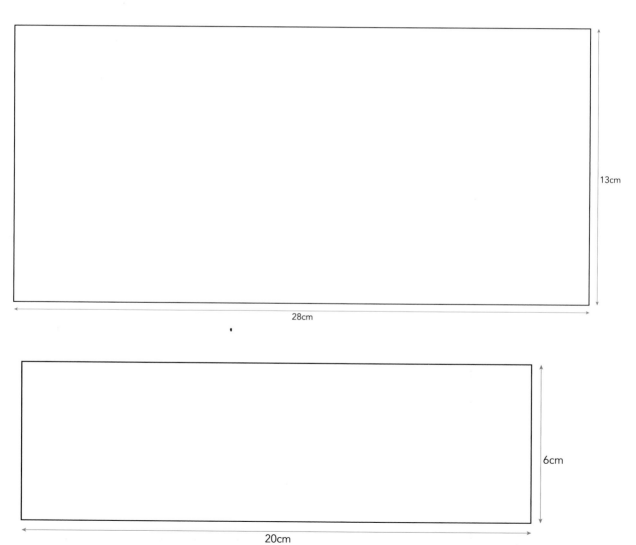

13cm

28cm

6cm

20cm

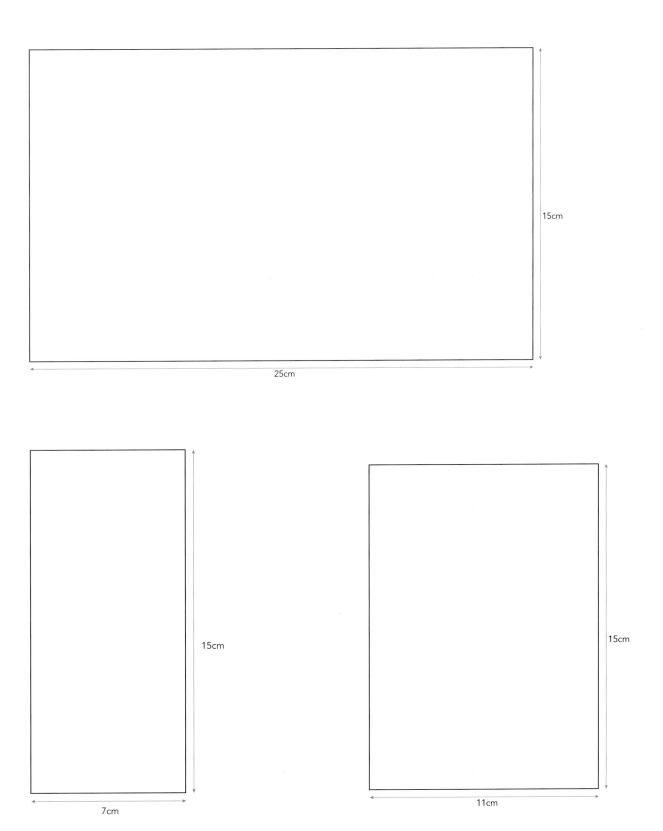

15cm

25cm

15cm

7cm

15cm

11cm

The Beach House

CONTINUES

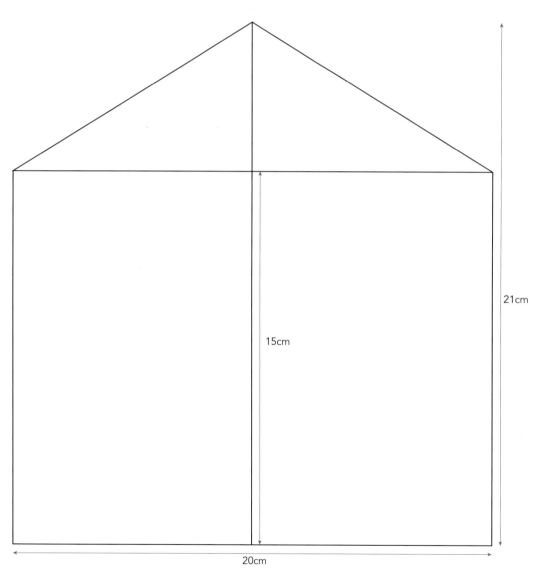

15cm

21cm

20cm

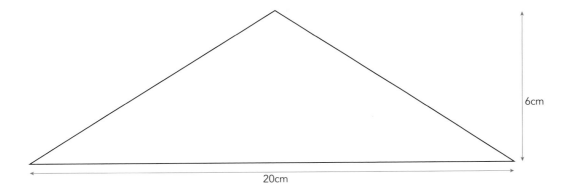

6cm

20cm

15cm

18cm

The Bird House

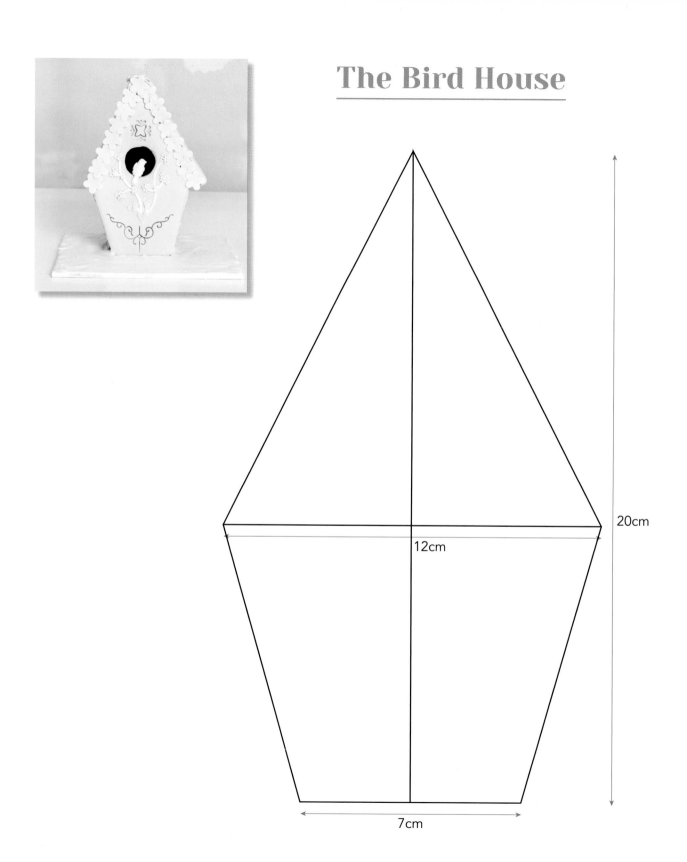

12cm

20cm

7cm

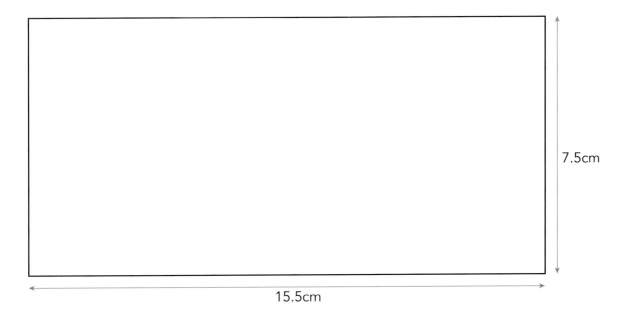

7.5cm

15.5cm

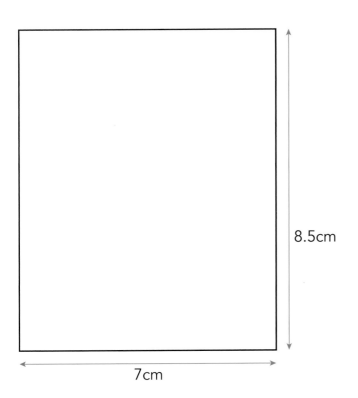

8.5cm

7cm

Cuckoo clock

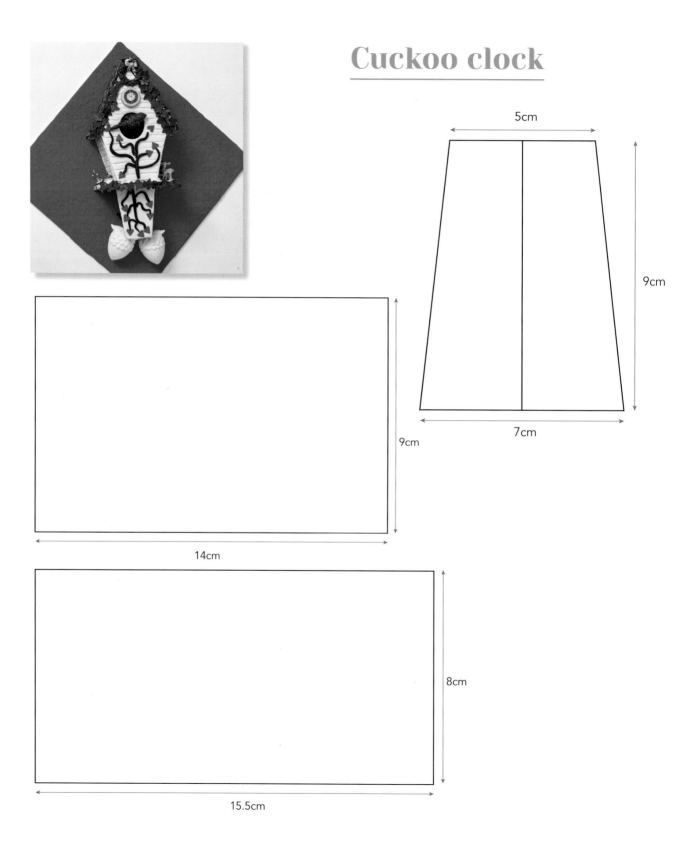

5cm

9cm

7cm

9cm

14cm

8cm

15.5cm

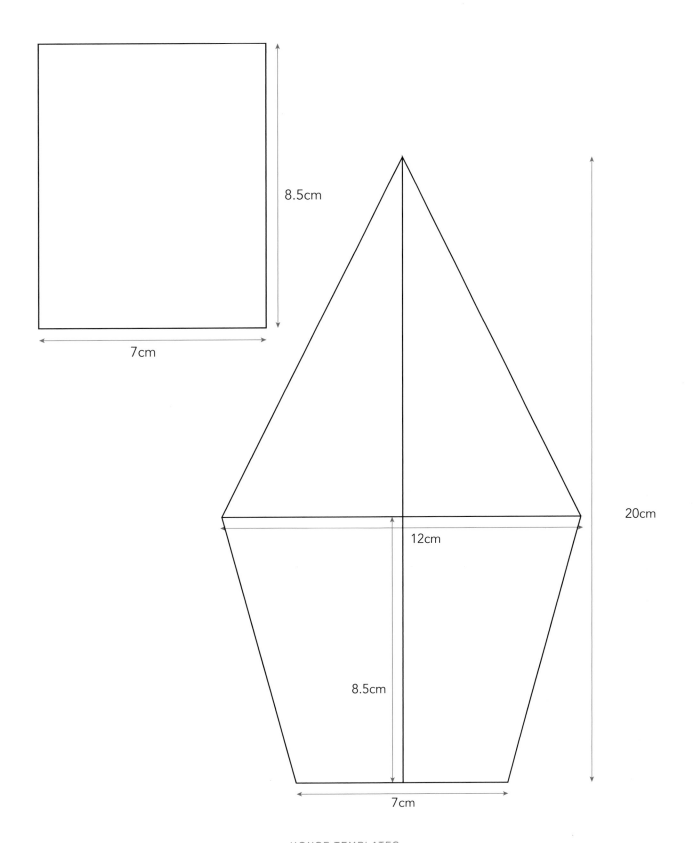

8.5cm

7cm

20cm

12cm

8.5cm

7cm

Modern Candy House

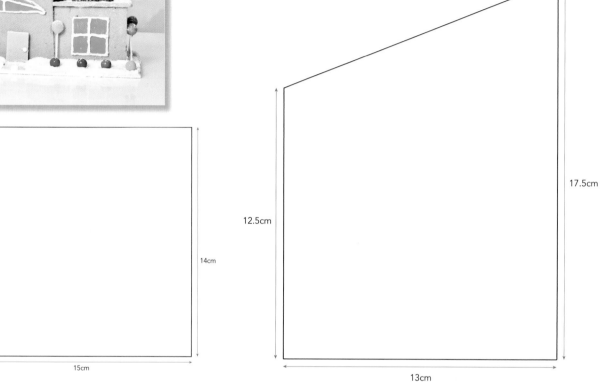

17.5cm

12.5cm

13cm

14cm

15cm

13cm

17.5cm

128

14cm

16cm

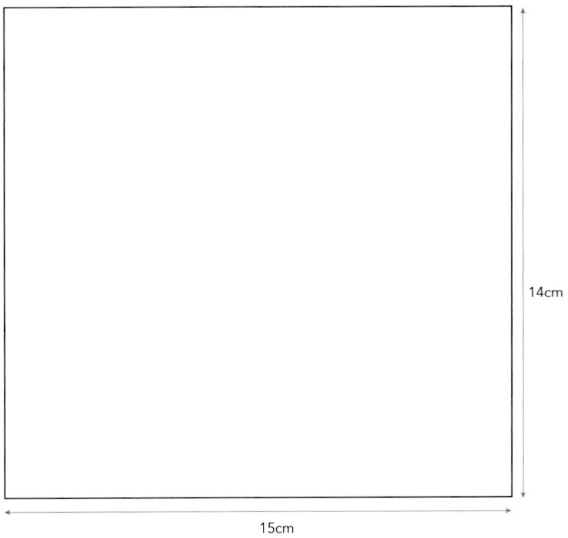

14cm

15cm

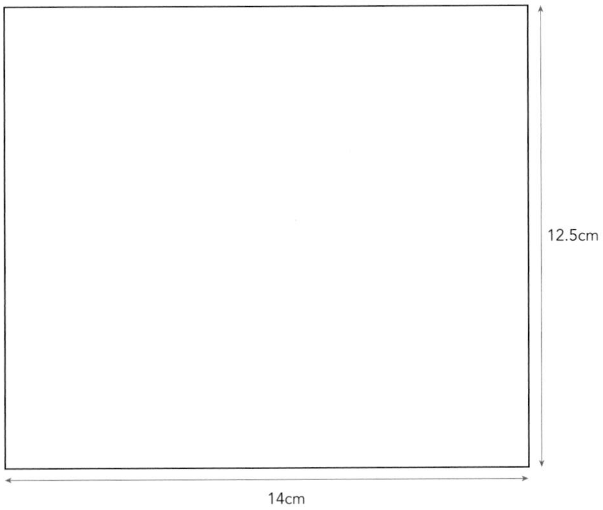

12.5cm

14cm

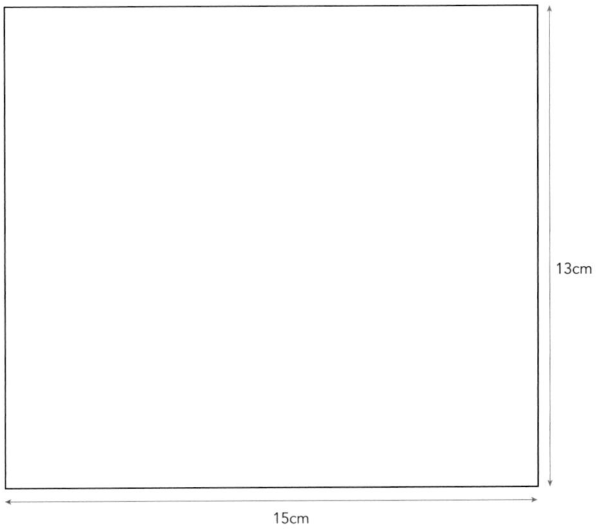

13cm

15cm

Caravan

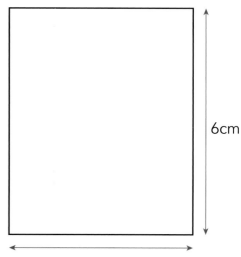

6cm

5cm

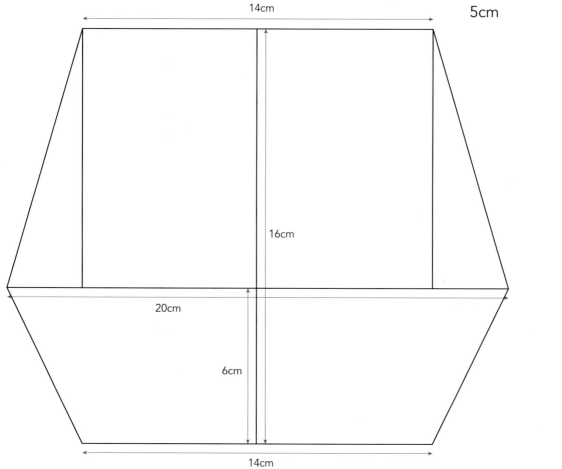

14cm

16cm

20cm

6cm

14cm

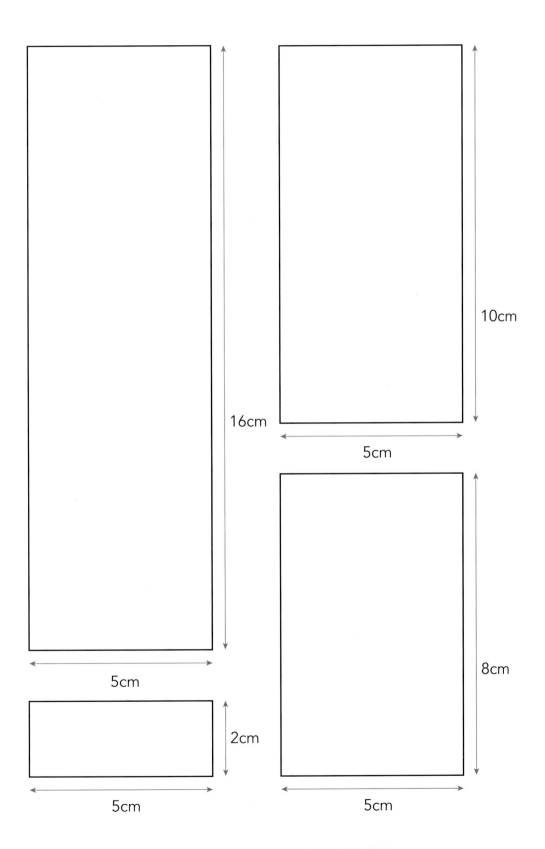

16cm

5cm

10cm

5cm

2cm

5cm

8cm

5cm

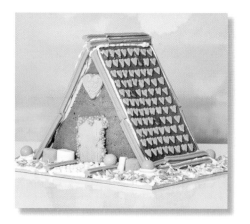

Pink Dollhouse

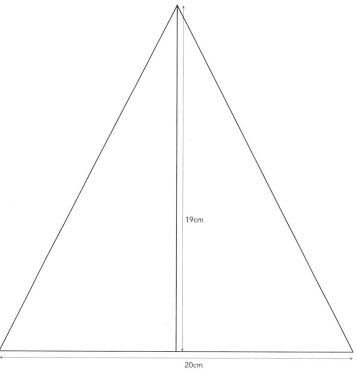

19cm

20cm

15cm

21cm

The School

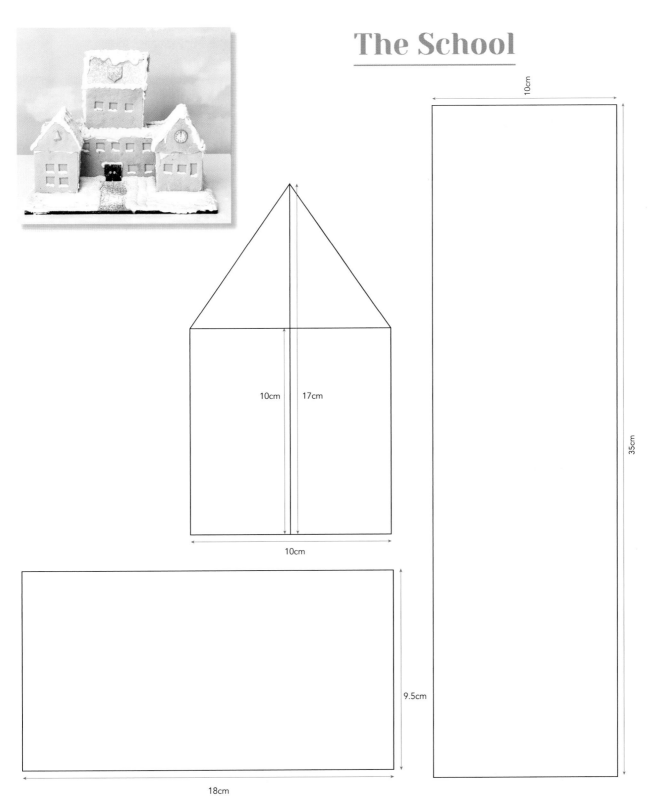

10cm

35cm

10cm

17cm

10cm

9.5cm

18cm

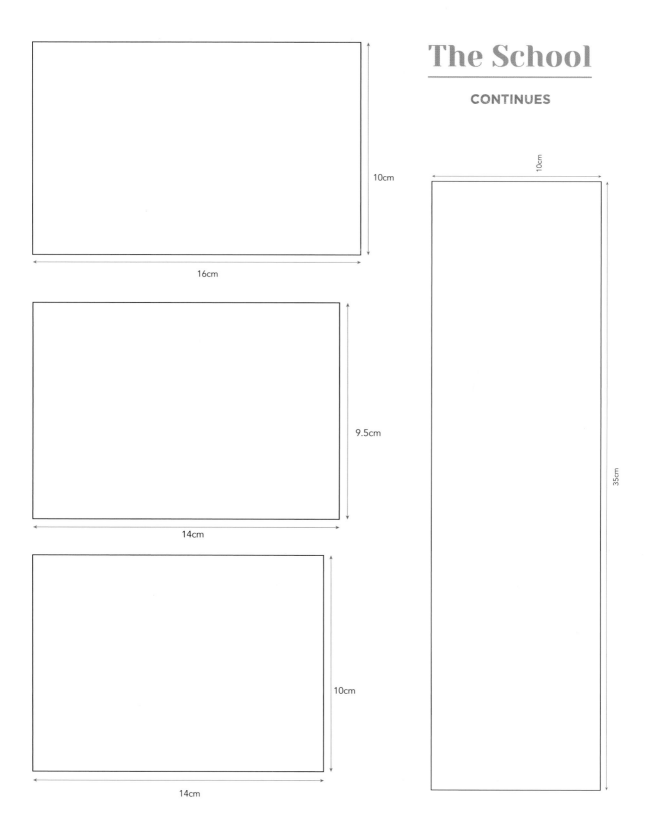

10cm

16cm

9.5cm

14cm

10cm

14cm

10cm

35cm

35cm

35cm

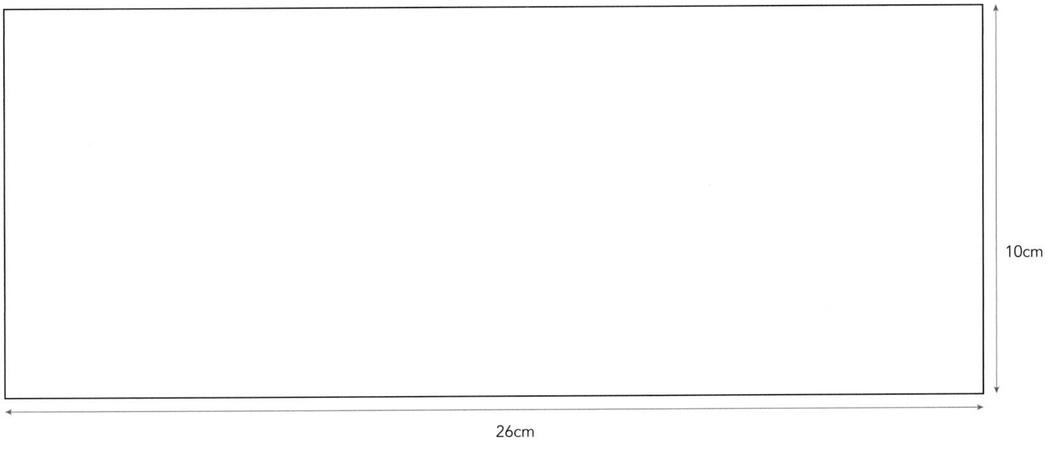

10cm

26cm

Beach Sheds

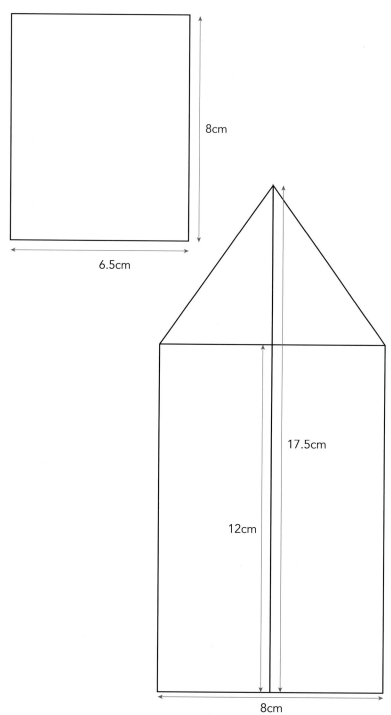

8cm

6.5cm

12cm

6cm

17.5cm

12cm

8cm

The Unit Block

20cm

13cm

22cm

22cm

Russian Dollhouse

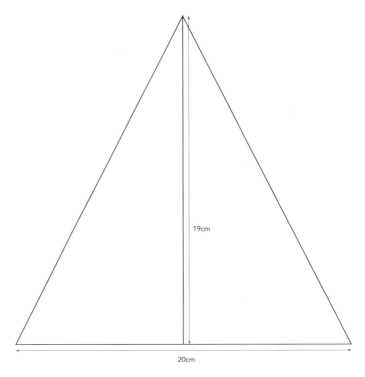

19cm

20cm

21cm

15cm

Compass to my heart

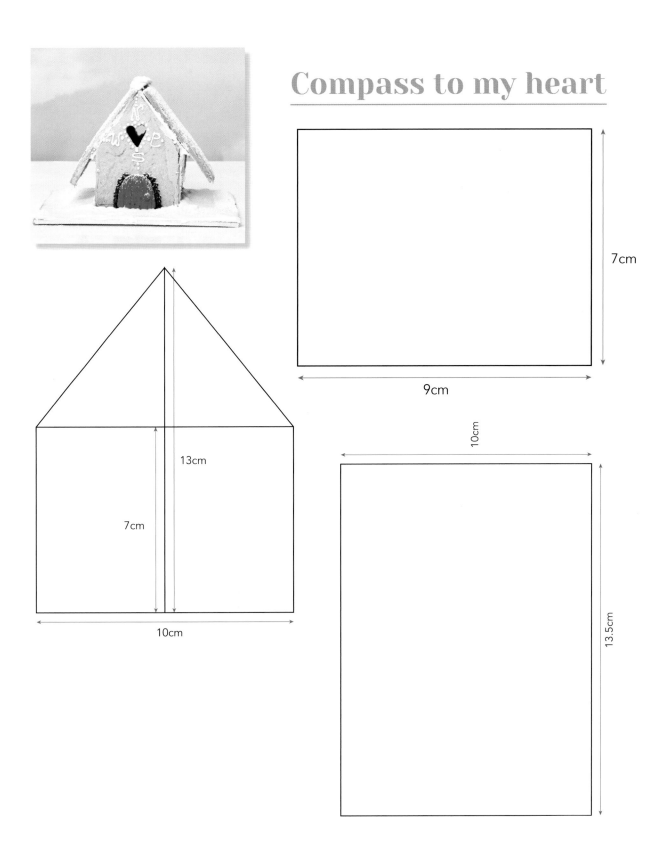

7cm

9cm

13cm

7cm

10cm

10cm

13.5cm

Small and Bright

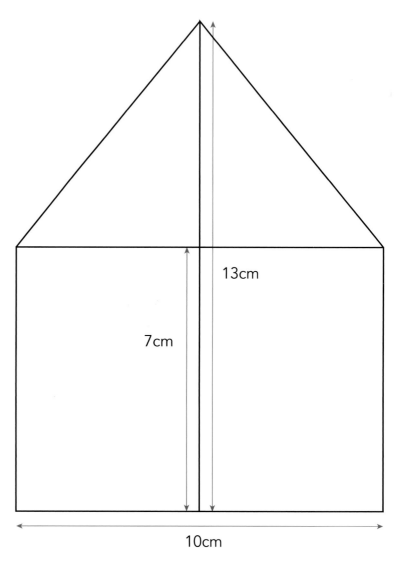

13cm

7cm

10cm

10cm

13.5cm

7cm

9cm

Easter Bunny House

HOUSE 1

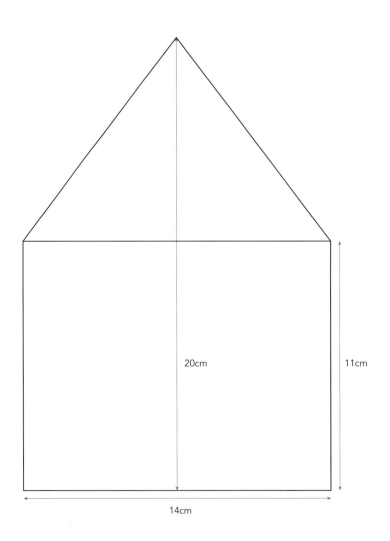

20cm

11cm

14cm

11cm

10cm

11cm

14cm

Easter Bunny House

HOUSE 2

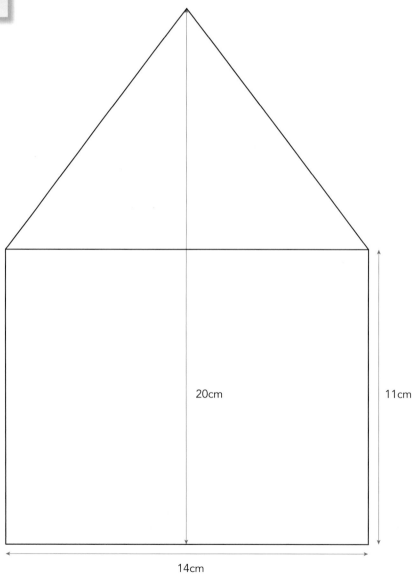

20cm

11cm

14cm

12cm

22cm

11cm

20cm

Log Cabin

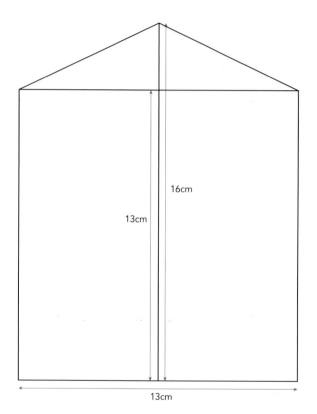

16cm

13cm

13cm

16cm

14cm

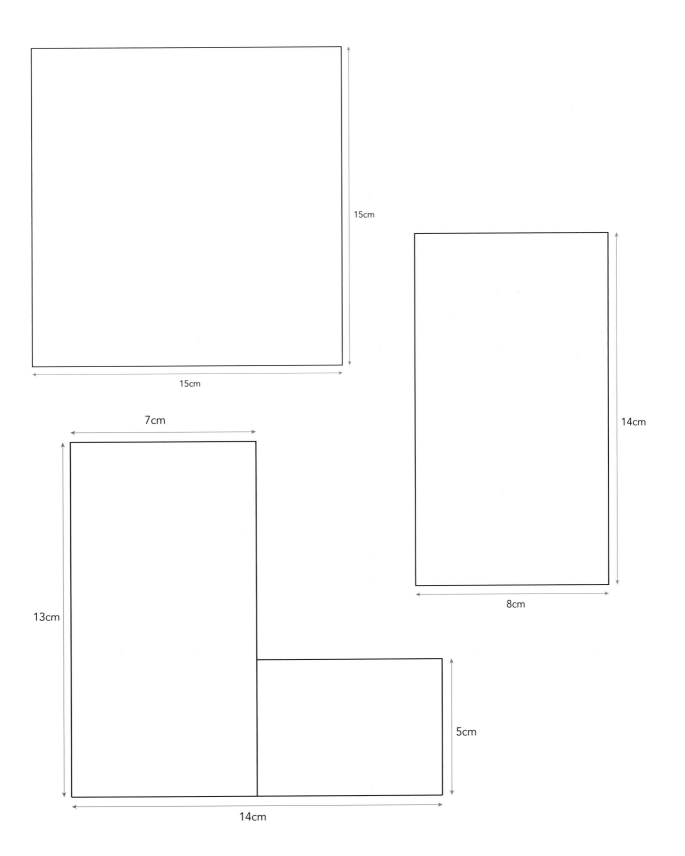

15cm

15cm

14cm

8cm

7cm

13cm

5cm

14cm

Ginger Townhouse Hill

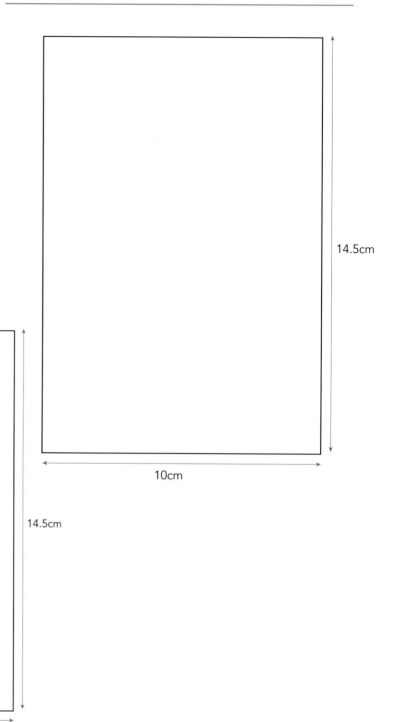

14.5cm

10cm

14.5cm

10cm

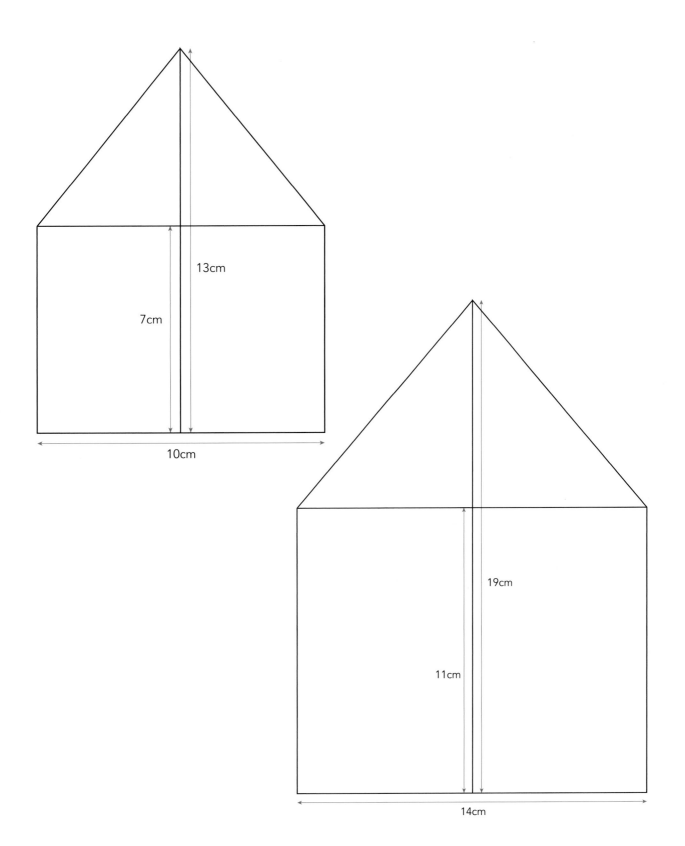

13cm

7cm

10cm

19cm

11cm

14cm

Hansel House

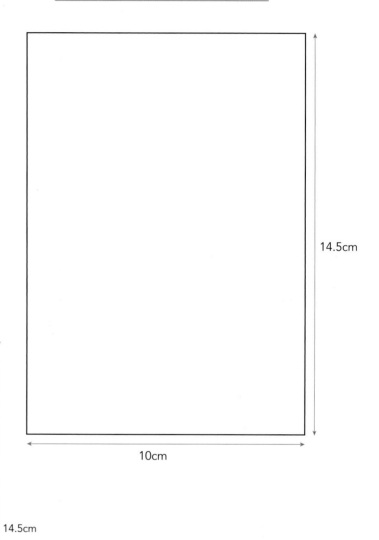

10cm

14.5cm

10cm

14.5cm

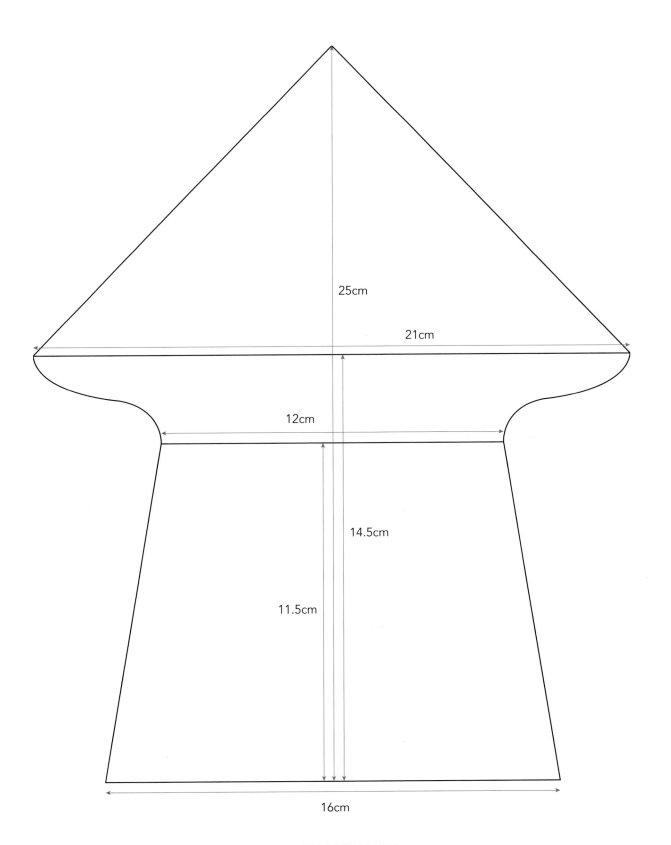

25cm

21cm

12cm

14.5cm

11.5cm

16cm

The Family Home

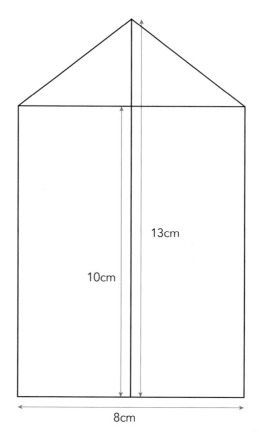

13cm

10cm

8cm

11cm

25cm

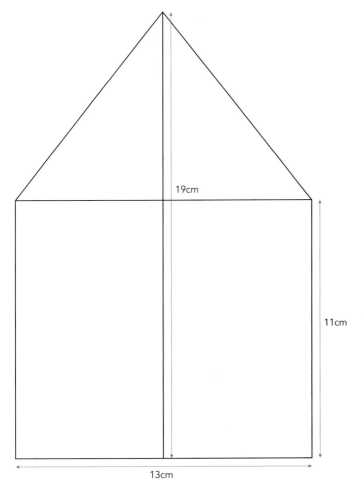

19cm

11cm

13cm

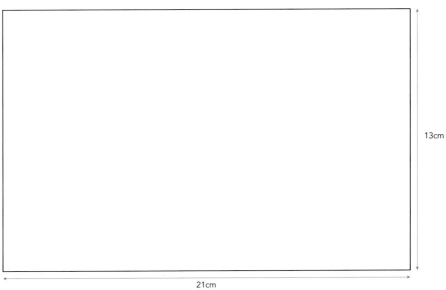

13cm

21cm

Fairy Garden

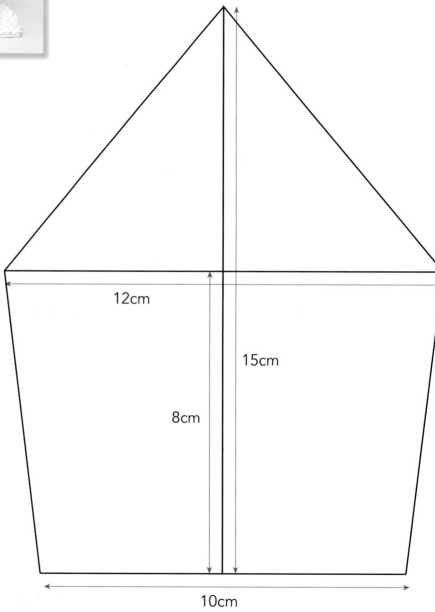

12cm

15cm

8cm

10cm

12.5cm

9cm

8.5cm

9cm

Chinese Garden

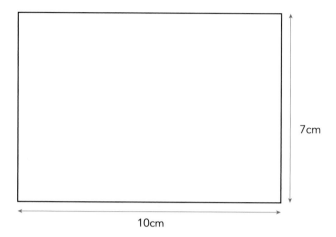

7cm

10cm

17cm

20cm

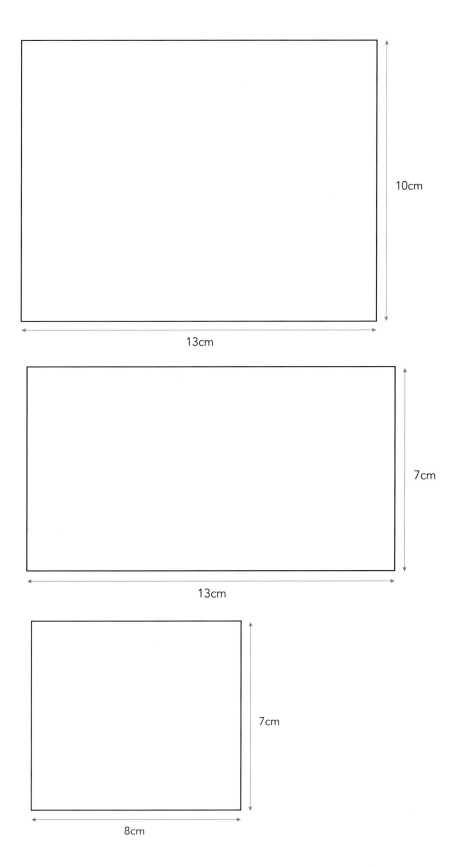

10cm

13cm

7cm

13cm

7cm

8cm

Chinese Garden

CONTINUES

12cm

15cm

7cm

15cm

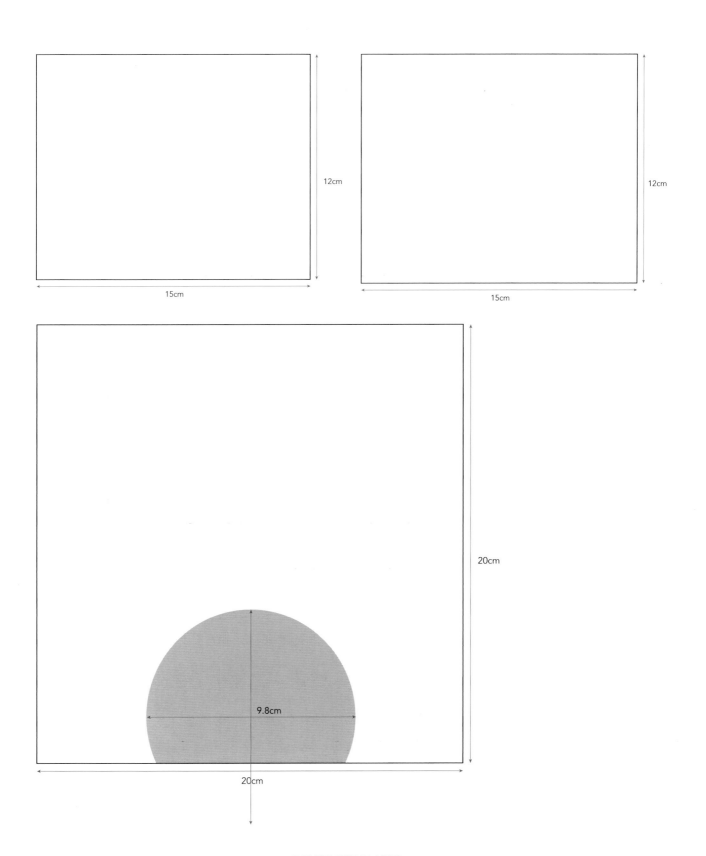

12cm

15cm

12cm

15cm

20cm

9.8cm

20cm

The Cake Shop

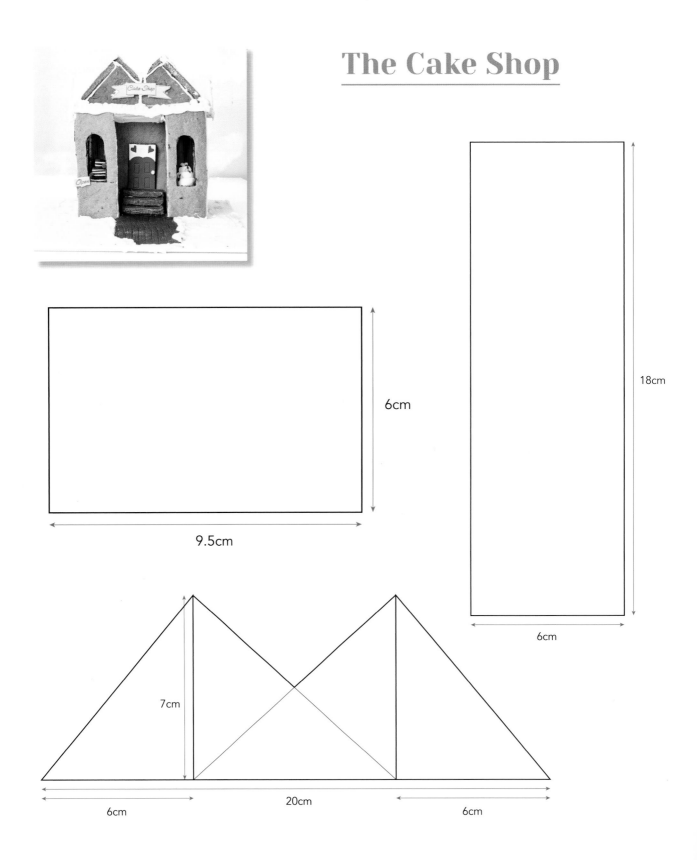

6cm

9.5cm

18cm

6cm

7cm

6cm

20cm

6cm

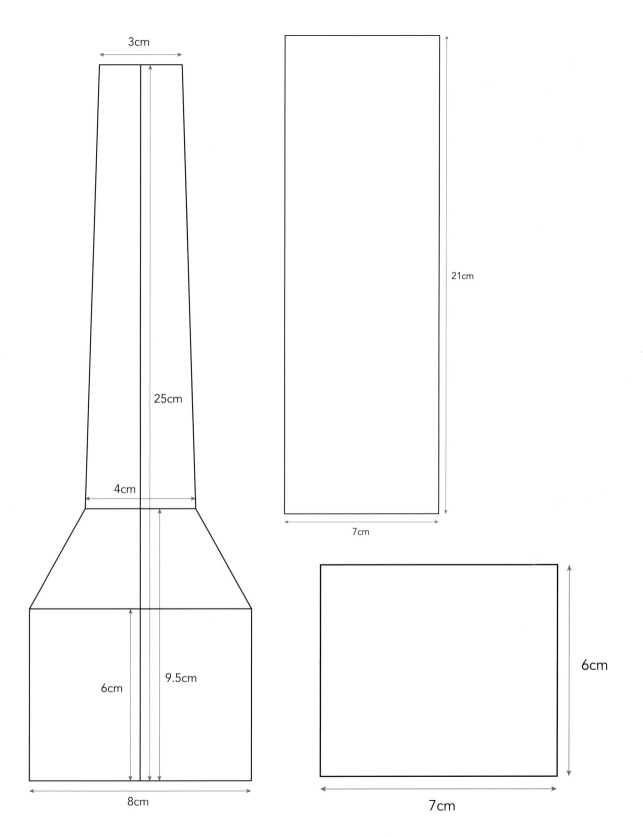

3cm

25cm

4cm

6cm

9.5cm

8cm

21cm

7cm

7cm

6cm

The Cake Shop

CONTINUES

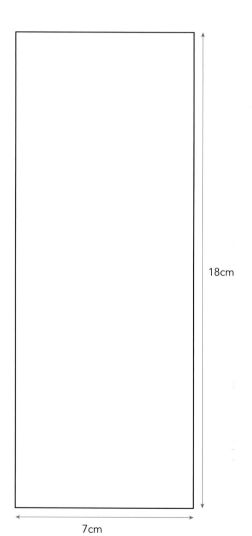

7cm

18cm

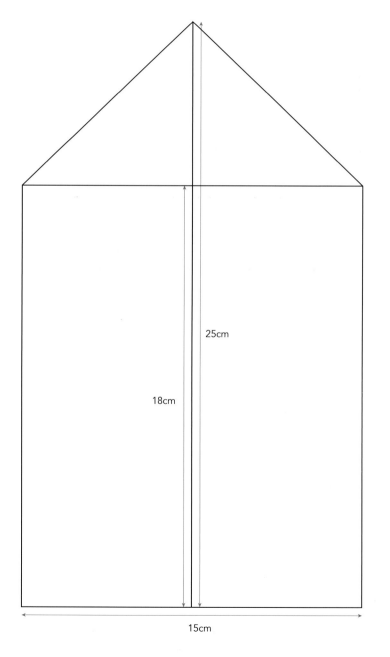

25cm

18cm

15cm

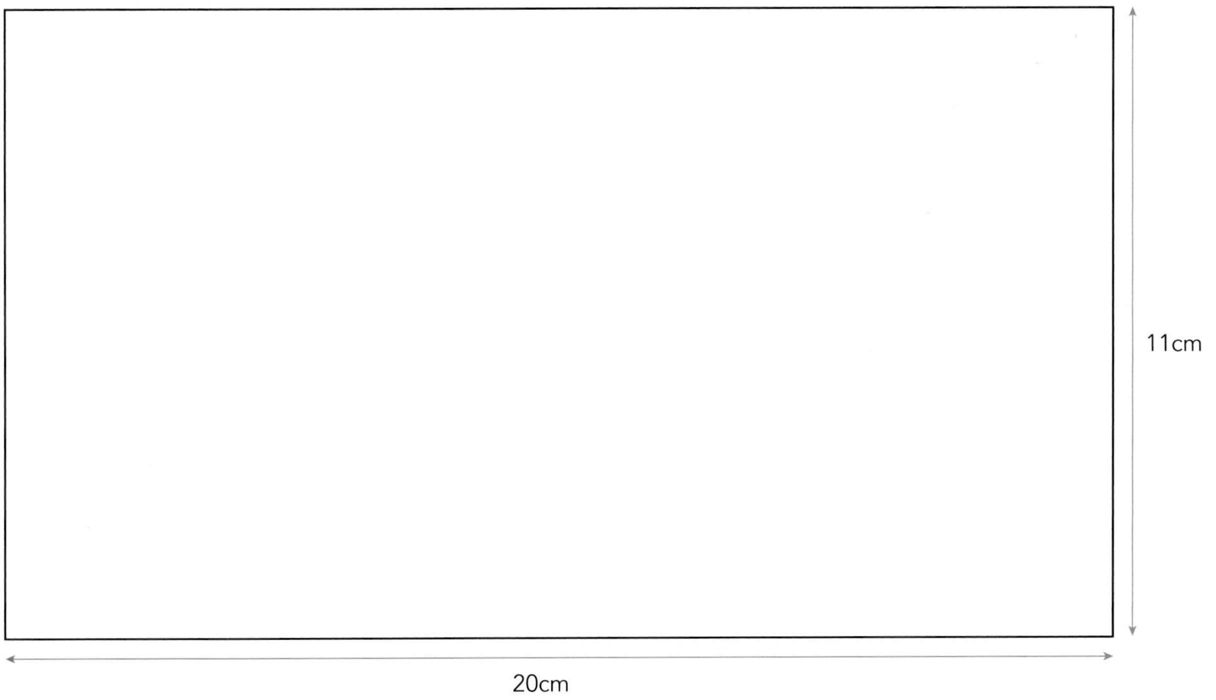

11cm

20cm

18cm

20cm

Lolly House

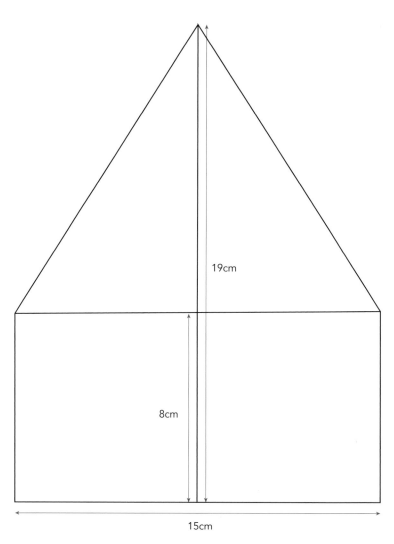

19cm

8cm

15cm

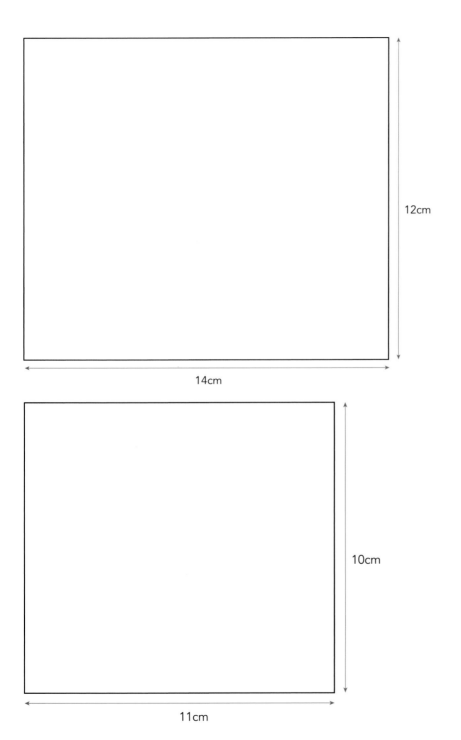

12cm

14cm

10cm

11cm

Simple Lolly House

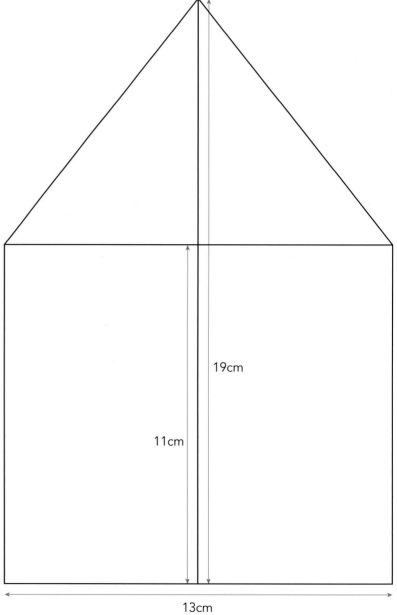

19cm

11cm

13cm

11cm

17cm

13cm

15cm

Mug Houses

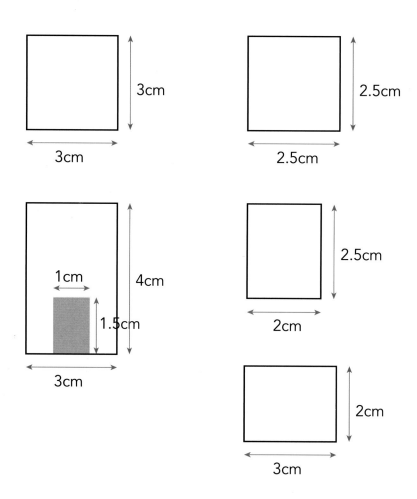

3cm

3cm

2.5cm

2.5cm

1cm

4cm

1.5cm

3cm

2.5cm

2cm

2cm

3cm

TeePee Mini and Maxi

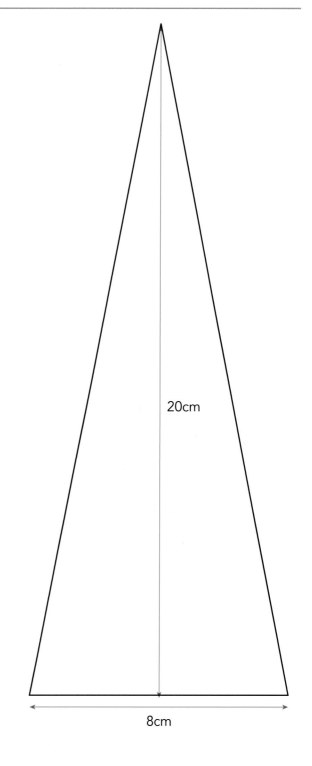

20cm

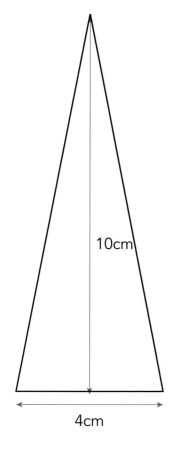

10cm

4cm

8cm

The Barn

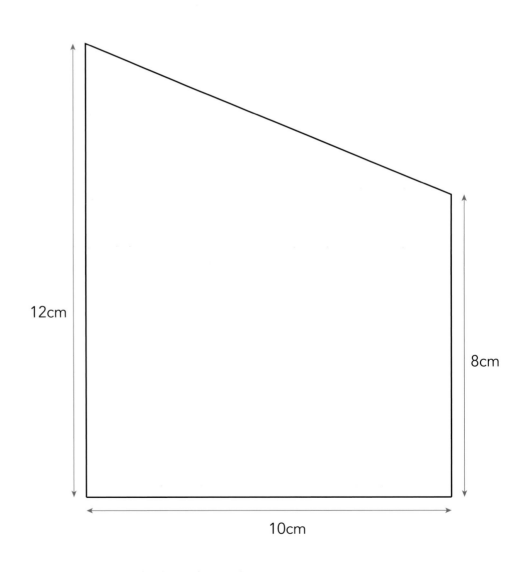

12cm

8cm

10cm

14cm

14cm

8cm

20cm

ACKNOWLEDGEMENTS

Thank you to New Holland Publishers for such a wonderful opportunity, I am so fortunate to work with such great people.

Thank you to Luke Olsen, owner of Cake Decorating Solutions Australia, it's a great place to work and has brilliant products. Majority of the tools used in this book were purchased here.

Cake lace mats used in this book are Crystal by Claire Bowman (http://www.cakelace.co.uk/) and the lace itself is both Claire Bowman Cake Lace and Flexilace (Cake Lace in Diamond White) (http://www.flexipaste.com/#flexipaste).

Thank you to Angela of the Sweet Spot Patisserie for answering many questions and being a great fact-checking source for this book. And to Jean Palmer for her lessons on how to make little birds, though I am sure no-one will ever make them as well as she does.

A big thank you to my family, especially my parents, Debbie and Gary, my Nan, and Gary and Angela, for all of their love, support and unwavering belief in me— like the backbone of life you keep me balanced and steady.

A special shout out to my boss, Tania Pantos, for all of her support and advice during the writing of this book. I'm very lucky to work among such talented people I can call friends.

For my friends; Andrew, Sarah, Maria, Lynda, Alex, Jo, Sarah, Jim, Jen, Jenny, Erin, Sue, Keri, Chris, Mat and Katty, thank you for putting up with me—being absent, being late and generally banging on about baking most of the time. Mostly, thank you for believing in me and encouraging me to take the leap. This book is also for you.

Most importantly—thank you to my husband for his on-going support, physical labor needed to complete this book and for generally living among gingerbread houses for months on end. I couldn't do any of this without your support my love, I am forever grateful.

First published in 2017 by New Holland Publishers
London • Sydney • Auckland

The Chandlery 50 Westminster Bridge Road London SE1 7QY United Kingdom
1/66 Gibbes Street Chatswood NSW 2067 Australia
5/39 Woodside Ave Northcote Auckland 0627 New Zealand

www.newhollandpublishers.com

A record of this book is held at the British Library and the National Library of Australia.

ISBN 9781742577777

Group Managing Director: Fiona Schultz
Publisher: Diane Ward
Project Editor: Kaitlyn Smith
Designer: Lorena Susak
Production Director: James Mills-Hicks
Printer in Malaysia by Times Offset (M) Sdn. Bhd.

10 9 8 7 6 5 4 3 2 1

Keep up with New Holland Publishers on Facebook
www.facebook.com/NewHollandPublishers